A GREEN MANIFESTO

A GREEN MANIFESTO

POLICIES FOR A GREEN FUTURE

SANDY IRVINE AND ALEC PONTON

FOREWORD BY JONATHON PORRITT

An OPTIMA book

First published in 1988 by
Macdonald Optima, a division of
Macdonald & Co. (Publishers) Ltd

A member of Maxwell Pergamon Publishing Corporation PLC

British Library Cataloguing in Publication Data

Irvine, Sandy
    A Green manifesto.
    1. Great Britain. Political parties.
    Green Party. Policies
    1. Title   II. Ponton, Alec
    324.241′097

    ISBN 0-356-15200-6

Macdonald & Co. (Publishers) Ltd
3rd Floor
Greater London House
Hampstead Road
London NW1 7QX

Illustrations by Nicola Haynes

Typeset in Century Schoolbook by Leaper & Gard Ltd
Printed and bound in Great Britain by
The Guernsey Press Co. Ltd
Guernsey, Channel Islands

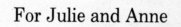
For Julie and Anne

CONTENTS

FOREWORD

There is little doubt that the electoral system in the UK has severely held back the development of Green politics; it remains extraordinarily difficult to persuade even those who are sympathetic to the Green cause that they are not 'wasting their vote' by casting it for a Green candidate, and this is unlikely to change until some version of proportional representation is introduced into this country.

Perhaps the most damaging knock-on effect of our 'winner-takes-all' electoral system has been the continuing difficulty of demonstrating at the *local* level the immediate relevance and viability of Green policies. For most people, politics means what's happening at that very moment in the Town Hall or Westminster, not the exchange of abstract principles and ideas. Endlessly to be saying what one would be doing, rather than actually to be doing it, makes it all too easy for cynics simply to dismiss new ideas as utopian or unrealistic. As this Manifesto so cogently reveals, any such cynicism about the burgeoning growth of the Greens throughout Europe would be wholly misplaced. Green politics is at last coming of age, and not before time. The body politic in the UK today is in a parlous state, kept ticking over on its life-support machine by recycled promises, short-term economic goodies, and precious raw materials culled from the Earth at a transparently unsustainable rate. Despite an illusion of life, it is all but brain-dead.

As the evidence of ecological disruption from around the world amply demonstrates, we are all living off borrowed time and borrowed wealth. It isn't easy to present this truth, the rock of political ecology, without falling into the old trap of an apocalyptic despair which merely disempowers those whom one seeks to reinvigorate. Nor is it easy to question prevailing assumptions about progress and what the future holds for us without sounding like some latter-day Luddite wanting to stop the world to drop off today's scientists and technologists. However, different interpretations of progress need to be questioned as rigorously as possible, for progress is indeed a questionable notion if it can only be achieved by irreparably breaching the finite limits of planet Earth.

There's a bare (but necessary!) modicum of doom and gloom in this particular Manifesto. But what makes Green politics so exciting today is the conviction that there really is a set of political principles both more equitable and realistic which will not entail everyone donning hair-shirts or sacrificing the 'good things' in life. Today's widespread patterns of alienation may well have moved beyond the reach of the simplistic politics of more and more, obliging us all to consider anew both the neglected political issues of community, solidarity and quality of life, as well as how best to free the human spirit. The *inner* limits that constrain the full potential of so many people are as blighting to the advance of humankind as our collective efforts to disregard the *outer* limits of the Earth's resources and life-support systems.

It's always good to discover a book that tells it as it is. The stark choice that Irvine and Ponton pose between mindless superindustrialism or a sustainable eco-society is one that we all have to face, reconciling as best we may the individual's so-called 'freedom of choice' with the rights of the dispossessed, future generations and the teeming multitude of other species with whom we share our earthly home. Even to face up to such dilemmas is something of a novelty in Mrs Thatcher's Britain, in that the opposition now seems incapable of articulating their visions without first genuflecting before the altar of increased economic growth and material affluence.

Better still, I imagine that this book will also ruffle a few feathers amongst the dozier inhabitants of the Green Party's own dovecote. Its uncompromising statement that issues like population and pollution matter a great deal more than the legalization of cannabis may not go down too easily in some quarters! Nor does that motley ever-expanding assembly of environmentalists escape unscathed, for Irvine and Ponton expose the very concept of contemporary environmentalism to a testing examination. As they rightly point out, there is indeed a thin line between taking up a long spoon to sup with the devils of today's industrial society and subsequently developing an unhealthy penchant for the succulent but subtly poisoned victuals set before one.

In the UK, as the authors readily acknowledge, the likelihood of a Green revolution with flags waving on the barricades is clearly somewhat remote. Even an electoral coup is hard to envisage in the short term. Yet time is desperately short, and anyone who cares about the Earth and about all its inhabitants should be deciding, even now, which side of these metaphorical barricades they would find themselves on.

A Green Manifesto will undoubtedly encourage those who still waver on the grounds of some perceived impracticality or narrow focus within Green politics. For this is emphatically *not* just another book about the state of the environment, detached from any social or political context. It is a hard-headed presentation of radical alternatives, based on a fundamental reinterpretation of the relationship between humankind and planet Earth. It provides us with an important staging post on the long Green march to a better future.

JONATHON PORRITT
1988

1.
POLITICS FOR LIFE

'Humanity has never been in a more critical situation in its entire history. We speak of this and that endangered species, but we do not seem to realize that we are perhaps the most endangered one.'

Professor Nicholas Georgescu-Roegen

These stark words come from one of the world's most distinguished economists and may well surprise many people. We have all become accustomed to the bland reassurances from politicians and other leading public figures that society's problems can be resolved by a mixture of hard work, incentives and technological ingenuity. Variations on this recipe form the staple diet of party manifestos around the world.

Professor Georgescu-Roegen is calling attention to a crisis which political organizations of left, right and centre seem unwilling to acknowledge. They remain steadfastly committed to policies which pander to the impossible dream of having our cake and eating it, apparently unconcerned that we are coming to the end of a period in history which can never be repeated. This has been described as the industrial growth society, and is

1

characterized by a relentless spread of urbanization and mass production. The accompanying explosion in environmental and social problems has created a situation which cannot last.

The difficulties of keeping a tottering show on the road have recently resurrected the politics of unashamed and ruthless self-interest. Its heartless and greedy values have not only swept through British politics, but have had widespread influence around the world. In countries like Australia, where equivalents of the British Labour Party hold power, it is often difficult to distinguish their policies from latter-day Conservatism. Even in some communist countries such as Hungary, the ruling bureaucrats are now expressing admiration for the much vaunted 'enterprise culture'.

In the richer countries, there is widespread support for this credo of 'self-first'. Many individuals seem driven by a desire to grab what they can for themselves. To some extent this may be reasonable — after all, most of us enjoy the occasional opportunity to indulge ourselves. However, some aspects of the acquisitive society such as the expansion of private healthcare and education reflect an underlying crisis of confidence. In the context of a crumbling social system, these developments are individual attempts to evade the issues. Private answers cannot solve public problems. The fanfares of the 'enterprise culture' are the last chords at the end of an era rather than the reveille for a brave new world.

We are close to the brink of destroying the conditions for human survival and that of other species. Contemporary industrial society is crushing the individual, local community and environment alike. People and places are being drawn into an ever more uniform lifestyle. In pursuit of the politics of 'moreness', governments of all shades are fast chipping away at civil liberties and local freedoms that stand in their way. Multinational corporations are tightening their stranglehold over our lives. New developments such as genetic engineering are removing the last restraints on manipulation. The true enemies of freedom are those who invoke its name in order that they may carry on without restraint.

Since the Second World War there has been mounting evidence of the dangerous direction in which society is heading. Starting with a trickle of books from far-sighted individuals, such as William Vogt, Fairfield Osborn, Samuel Ordway and Rachel Carson, it turned into a flood of conferences, studies and formal reports from a variety of prestigious bodies. Many have become well-known — *Limits to Growth* (1972), *Blueprint for Survival* (1972), the *Global 2000 Report to the President* (1980), *World Conservation Strategy* (1980), the *Brandt Report* (1983)

and the *Brundtland Report* (1987). These general surveys have
been complemented by a host of well-documented publications
and television programmes on specific issues from acid rain to
spreading deserts, from the crisis in healthcare to torture and
political persecution. Such evidence led Fritz Schumacher to
castigate politicians, claiming they merely wanted to rearrange
the deck chairs on the *Titanic*. He realized that the depth and
breadth of the predicaments facing society demand a fundamental change in the way we live.

Green politics are based on this reality. Already there are
signs of a small but growing shift in people's values and lifestyles; more and more individuals share Schumacher's concern.
It has been reflected in the rapid growth of all kinds of pressure
groups campaigning over issues such as disarmament, environmental protection and human rights. In response, major political
parties, some of which now contain environmental 'ginger'
groups, have begun to incorporate some of the ideas from this
broad movement — an encouraging development, but so far the
evidence suggests that a shade of Green is being used to camou-
flage the unchanged goals of traditional politics. From Left to
Right, manifestos are packed with policies that negate Green
principles.

The political debate currently revolves around false assumptions concerning the nature of the crisis facing society. Despite
all the arguments about the level of public spending or state
ownership versus privatization, traditional politicians agree that
society needs to accelerate out of trouble: more production, more
complex technology, more cost-effectiveness, bigger markets . . .
These are the wrong answers resulting from the wrong questions.

Greens have sought to separate surface symptoms from the
root causes of our growing problems. They have spotlighted the
direction society must take if it wants a sustainable and satisfying future: partnership with the rest of nature, 'soft' technology, 'steady-state' economics, human-scale institutions and a
population size within the environment's long-term carrying
capacity. One of the aims of this book is to introduce and explain
these ideas to a wider audience.

Though Green parties are only a few years old, they have
begun to translate principles into practicable policies. In this
book, we seek to make a modest contribution to this process and
hope to stimulate serious debate. We have tried to disentangle
the essential from the trivial. When the very habitability of the
Earth is under threat, it is absurd to dwell on minor issues such
as the legalization of cannabis or the future of the monarchy.
First things must come first!

The great issue of our time is resolving the crisis that has arisen between human society and the rest of the environment. All policies must be judged in terms of their contribution to getting this primary relationship right. The starting point of Green politics is the dependence of human beings on the ecological well-being of the Earth. Its policies reassert this vital relationship respecting the rights both of future generations and other species. In doing so, it seeks to create the conditions for peace, social justice and a flowering of a rich diversity of lifestyles and environments. A Green political manifesto is for *all* forms of life on Earth.

2.
THE ROAD TO RUIN

Many of us have seen the TV series and films about the voyage of the *Starship Enterprise*. Captain Kirk and his crew are a happy and healthy bunch whose only problems stem from encounters with hostile aliens, repeatedly overcome thanks to human ingenuity and the wonders of technological gadgetry. The American Dream has been fulfilled and *Enterprise* cruises through the galaxies, dispensing synthetic sweetness and light.

Sad to say, the inhabitants of our 'spaceship', the Earth, can rely on no such guarantee of a happy ending. We humans are not alone: we share the planet with myriad other species. All of us depend inescapably upon the well-being of the Earth. Yet human society, just one part of the Earth's community, is threatening not only itself but all of the rest as well. Through sheer numbers and the power of technology, human activity has become a malignant cancer draining the vitality of the Earth, creating a lethal imbalance between people and planet. Too often we abuse both basic human nature and its essential needs, pitting person against person in destructive competition.

Symptoms of this sickness dominate the daily news — terrorism, famine, war and weapons, superpower rivalry, religious extremism, racial conflict, violent crime, extremes of wealth and poverty, unemployment, pollution, threats to wildlife ... the list seems endless. To make matters worse, these symptoms feed off each other. The Earth, simply as a dead rock, is for all intents and purposes indestructible, but unless we change course human society faces self-destruction, taking many other life-forms with it.

FALSE ALARMS?

Prophecies of doom have been proved wrong many times before, yet some societies in the past *have* committed ecological suicide. Fortunately it has always been restricted in scale and impact; today the problem is global. Crisis could come in the big bang of nuclear suicide, but it is more likely to be the slow process of environmental degradation. Though we cannot predict events exactly, we know that whatever happens in the short term we are becoming increasingly trapped in a spiral of destruction. There is yet hope, however. As the American ecologist Kenneth Watt comments, 'the magnitude of disasters decreases to the extent that people believe that they are possible, and plan to prevent them, or to minimize their effects.' We believe that the time for action is now.

ALL THAT GLITTERS ...

Conventional politics resolutely turns the other way in the face of such bad tidings. Governing parties are particularly fond of telling the public that they have never had it so good. The opposition parties dispute this, but only on the grounds that they can deliver more goods. They never question either the ecological sustainability or the moral desirability of the industrial system itself.

It is not difficult to see why this faith in business-as-usual has many believers, especially in rich Western countries. Here even the poorest people are comparatively privileged in terms of basic security and creature comforts. General consumer spending continually reaches new heights: strawberries may be eaten in winter, and for many central heating is a blanket against the cold; holiday brochures announce exotic locations, while TV and video bring a semblance of the world into our living room. More people are receiving more schooling. Every area of life now has its specialists to minister to our needs. Yesterday's science fiction becomes today's fact as technology performs miracles ranging from surgery to space stations. Endless statistics take the place of knowledge and wisdom.

However, the structures of the industrial growth society are beginning to fall apart.

...IS NOT GOLD

We may not see many scars of absolute poverty in the industralized world, yet problems are piling up within our society; mental illness, cancer and heart disease, the divorce rate, child abuse, racial and sexual discrimination, occupational hazards, the care of the aged, crumbling public services, the ugliness and congestion of our surroundings, government secrecy, homelessness, house prices, the boredom and futility of many jobs, low pay and long-term unemployment are just a few of the symptoms.

If societies like Britain are skating on thin ice, others are falling through holes in the surface. One billion people across the Third World live in desperate poverty. In the next 60 seconds, 30 children will die from lack of food and adequate health care.

However, the deepest cracks are opening outside human society, where our centuries of exploiting nature are fast approaching a violent climax. Acid rain, holes in the ozone layer, topsoil erosion, the greenhouse effect, disappearing jungles and extinct wildlife are examples of an assault against the Earth itself.

TURNING A BLIND EYE

Many of us do not heed these signs at all. For many, the sheer pressure of 'getting on' with the routines of everyday life blots out deeper issues. Others may see the dangers, but feel helpless. Some genuinely cannot see what it has got to do with them, while yet others say 'eat, drink and be merry ...' Most worrying of all are those in rich and poor countries alike who, protected by their own wealth, ignore or make excuses for the suffering around them.

The industrial growth society is built upon exploitation within societies, between societies, and between humans and other species. The ones who suffer are those who find themselves in the way of technological 'progress'. There is also the vicious exploitation of 'guest workers'. Internationally, a global underclass is being expelled into marginal lands or shanty towns to make way for more plantations, more ranches, more mining, tourist developments, and not least because of endemic warfare. Traditional tribal peoples are being driven from their lands into cultural, if not physical, oblivion.

And the price is not just human. Various pressure groups have rightly drawn attention to the cruelty of intensive livestock units, fur farms, zoos, circuses and research laboratories. Equally appalling is the destruction of wildlife habitats and the extinction of species after species. At the same time, more and more of the Earth itself is being buried alive under tarmac and concrete, destroyed by intensive farming or drowned beneath impounded water.

Many short-term winners in this dog-eat-dog life vote for politicians who unashamedly promise to enrich the rich. Behind the façades of government, even in the few representative democracies, are the self-perpetuating clandestine organizations. They may be official, such as 'security' agencies, or unofficial, such as the Trilateral Commission, a club of international business executives, financiers, politicians and media personnel. The latter typifies a number of organizations devoted to preserving the ascendancy of industrial capitalism in the rich countries of the world. The ruling élites of the communist world are in practice little different, and in this battleground of ideas, the so-called New Enlightenment resurrects old rationales for inequality and discrimination, spreading a veil of darkness over true wisdom and compassion.

In the long run it will make little difference. Eventually even the high ground of society will be engulfed by the rising waters of ecological instability.

CRASHING THROUGH THE SAFETY BARRIERS

How has this dangerous situation come about? What are the forces driving humanity down the wrong road?

In essence the problem can perhaps best be seen as the inevitable consequence of not living within natural limits. Everything has its limits, from the organs of our bodies to entire ecosystems — they act as brakes on harmful excess. No part of any system — of a plant, animal, community, institution, machine or environment — can grow indefinitely, displacing other parts. First it would disrupt, then it would destroy, the whole system, itself included.

Today human numbers and human technologies appear to be causing precisely this sort of disruption, in society and to the broader environment. We alone, of all species, have been able to override nature's brakes on excessive growth and imbalance. Now we are crashing through one safety barrier after another.

OUT OF ORDER

When it is tired or unwell a human body gives out appropriate signals. So too do social and environmental systems. Symptoms ranging from dying forests and spreading deserts to social disorders of every kind are telling us that we must reassess our ways; that we are failing to live within the rhythms, tolerances and capabilities of nature, not least those of our own physiological and psychological nature.

We are overstretching our inner limits of mind and body. We are expecting too much of machines and gadgetry. We are overtaxing our capacities to manage. Most dangerously, we are placing too many demands on the foundations of life, those ecological processes by which nature sustains, repairs and regulates itself. This is not some hypothetical 'balance' in the sense of a fixed and stationary point; what concerns us is the loss of resilience, the ability of individuals, communities and environments to cope with change.

Complete disorder is the inevitable consequence of placing too many demands on people and planet alike, demands which are overwhelming in both scale and kind. They result from excesses in:

- Human numbers.
- Human technologies and the extent and intensity of their systems.
- Human institutions, especially economies that are dependent on the overconsumption of physical space and natural resources, with a 'big is beautiful' approach in business, welfare and governmental institutions.
- The one-sidedness of a culture which fragments reality, devaluing all that cannot be precisely measured and quantified, and which has an obsession with control and subjugation. The result is that thinking is divorced from feeling, and nature is viewed as an enemy to be harnessed and exploited.

Taken separately, these forces might not seem very threatening. What is so deadly, however, is their interaction, and the way in which they multiply each other's effects. Together they are tearing away the fabric of society and environment. Together they are robbing both future generations and other living species of what is rightfully theirs. Together they constitute a serious evolutionary crisis.

SHOULDERING THE RESPONSIBILITY

These then are the key driving forces pushing humanity down the wrong road. But an important question is still left begging: who *is* responsible? We are fond of blaming 'them' (and asking 'why don't they do something about it?'). Most radical analysts will say that 'they' do indeed exist, in the form of powerful

9

vested interests controlling the institutions of society, pursuing their own goals regardless of the consequences. The resultant socio-economic structures often leave the individual with little choice. This is seen at its most cruel when the world's poor are driven to destroy their tomorrow in a desperate attempt to survive today.

Most radical analyses stop here, failing to grasp the whole picture. Nevertheless, we must also recognize how individual decision-making contributes to our collective problems. These are not only the result of major institutional decisions; they are also the cumulative consequences of all those little choices we each make, so seemingly insignificant in themselves but so destructive in total. Most of us do not want more congestion, more urban sprawl, more pollution, more extinction of wildlife, yet we all help it to take place.

The dynamics of the situation make it difficult for individuals to foresee the long-term, aggregate results of how they decide to live. Moreover, the disadvantages of changing our ways often outweigh the personal benefit we might derive, and it seems pointless if everyone else continues as before. In small-scale societies, cultural factors such as social customs and taboos contributed towards making group members observe their responsibilities. In a mass society with the might of technology at its disposal, this divorce between the individual and the collective good threatens to be fatal for all concerned.

Nothing illustrates this better than overpopulation. Consider, for example, an affluent couple in a country such as Britain. They might want an extra child for all kinds of personally valid reasons. If they go ahead, it makes a negligible difference to population increase and their wishes are fulfilled. If they decide not to go ahead, they forego the pleasures that an extra child could have brought and, since other couples continue to have children, their abstinence seems to be pointless. The example spotlights how many people who are well aware of the problems chronicled in this book and are able to exercise choice in their lives, nevertheless parent large families.

This, more than any other factor, explains why social change cannot be left solely to individual action. It must be part of a concerted political programme which seeks to change both our institutions, and the values they embody.

3.
LIVING WITHIN LIMITS

Far from being irksome restrictions, limits ensure that life can continue to flourish.

Unlike others, the Green approach takes this as its starting point, and it is here that Green thinking cuts most sharply against the grain of conventional wisdom. The values we support — modesty, gentleness and spiritual development, for example — clash with the aggressive, egotistical and materialistic beliefs which dominate today's society. Our thinking is at odds with what can be seen as the religion of progress, a modern opiate of the people.

This faith takes many forms. It ranges from dreams of a world of material abundance to a belief that technology might one day even conquer death itself. Where there's a will, there's sure to be a way: any obstacles will simply be overcome by the appliance of science, by managerial expertise, or by the economic system (through more profit incentives or more planning).

Ecologist David Ehrenfeld, in his notable book *The Arrogance of Humanism*, observes that one deep-seated reason for the popularity of corny space fiction such as *Star Trek* is that it reflects and feeds this faith, highlighting the possibility of more of whatever we want. It also explains the sometimes hysterical response to the famous *Limits to Growth* report to the Club of Rome which challenged the whole basis of society's current direction by using computers, a technology to which the high priests of endless progress and their followers ascribe almost magical powers.

UTOPIA UNLIMITED

The ideology of expansionism pervades modern society. Most of our institutions are rooted in what economist Herman Daly calls 'growthmania'. It is not confined to the business world. Schools and colleges measure their success in terms of more students, more courses, more promoted posts and so forth. We see politicans of Left, Right and Centre competing over who can bake the biggest cake. Communist governments pledge they will catch up with and surpass the levels of material consumption in capitalist countries. Third World leaders vow to bring the life-styles of the rich North to all corners of the globe. Advertising agencies milk the dream for all it is worth. Many children's books about life in the future portray a world whose inhabitants (when not visiting other planets) seem to enjoy endless leisure, served by an array of gadgets that cater for their every need. Publications like Julian Simon's *The Resourceful Earth* show that these infantile fantasies are not the sole property of the young.

Few would categorically deny that one day we will have to call a halt. Most devote their time instead to a denial that these limits have any meaning for today's decisions.

THE END OF A DREAM

The cornucopian faith will probably be short-lived. Though its roots may be traced to that period of European intellectual history known as the Enlightenment, it has only flowered fully in the last hundred years. It is doubtful whether it will survive into the next century. The limits to growth — of population, economic production and technological innovation — are not the invention of malevolent 'econuts', rather a phenomenon that we ignore at our peril. We all know our bodies do not continue to grow, and our minds can cope with only so many demands. We never have time for all the things we would like to do. Such limits to the size and rate of growth apply to all aspects of life. We must acknowledge the constraints upon further expansion, and the intolerable costs of ignoring them.

At one extreme are the 'outer' limits defined by the biological and physical constraints of our environment. At the other lie the 'inner' limits of human psychology and physiology. Together, they are the basis of what William Ophuls calls 'ecological scarcity'.

The three key limits might be called the three E's — Earth, entropy and ecology. Obviously the Earth is limited in sheer physical space, and this restricts the location, quantity and accessibility of the various resources we require. There are limits to what we can tap from so-called renewable resources as much as from non-renewable ones. Entropy and ecology are rather more difficult concepts, and will be considered later (see p. 26).

THE LIMITS OF MORALITY

There is one further constraint, which we may feel free to ignore because it concerns ethics. Why shouldn't this generation echo the old Bourbon kings of France in proclaiming: 'After us, the deluge!'? Marxists used to talk about the 'inevitability of socialism' (and some still do). Greens derive no such comfort. Society can indeed live as if there were no tomorrow. Any other destination will only be reached by conscious choice.

These ethical limits include the creation of intolerable risks to third parties from hazardous and polluting technologies; the exploitation of non-human species and the destruction of their habitats; the robbing of what future generations will need through resource depletion and environmental degradation by those alive today. We do not have to pay attention to such limits, but failure to do so can cut us off from the richest part of our humanity.

LIMITS UNLIMITED

These various limits interact. We have only mentioned the more obvious, omitting those less predictable ones such as disruptive changes in weather patterns. What matters is not any particular limit, which might be overcome, but the total interaction of constraints, and costs. Combined they suggest that the industrial growth society is doomed. Continued attempts to maintain it will produce increasingly negative trade-offs, with diminishing returns in all areas of life.

Declining quality in our lives might encourage people to call a halt to further overall expansion. There is nothing to stop us gaining more satisfaction and happiness, from less goods and services. In a new 'steady-state', things would not be static; some would expand while others contracted. But overall, our culture, our technologies, our political and economic systems, must be rooted in the checks and balances of life on Earth. And the sooner we begin to make the transition, the better for all concerned.

4.
SOME BASIC PRINCIPLES

Greens are guided by four fundamental assumptions. These are that:
- Life on Earth should continue.
- Human life on Earth should continue.
- Natural justice should be done.
- There is a quality of life worth pursuing independent of material well-being.

From these we can derive a number of working principles, to guide both individual and collective action. Given the political focus of this book, they are framed within the context of governmental power, but we hope that individuals and pressure groups will find them useful. We have tried to put them in some sort of rough order, and would stress that they should be treated as a stimulus, not as absolute dogma.

PUT EARTH FIRST
Above all else, maintain and respect the integrity and viability of nature's life-supporting and life-enhancing ecosystems.

LIVE WITHIN LIMITS
We do not create wealth. We can live off the 'interest' of nature's bounty, but it is self-defeating to squander her 'capital'.

Further, there are limits to expansion which, if transgressed, can only bring diminishing returns and potential disaster.

THINK IN TERMS OF SUFFICIENCY
An attitude of 'enough' must replace that of 'more'.

TREAD LIGHTLY
In living we all place demands upon each other, society and other forms of life. Killing and suppression are a part of nature, but should be restricted to meeting our essential needs. All species share the basic right to exist simply because they exist. We must seek productive coexistence, treading lightly in all these relationships.

DEFEND DIVERSITY
There is intrinsic merit in the rich variety and complexity of environment and culture. This must be defended against increasing uniformity.

RESPECT OUR DESCENDANTS' RIGHTS
We are obliged to pass on to future generations an environment and culture which is as safe, rich and varied as possible.

DESIGN WITH NATURE
Through evolution, a process of trial and error, nature has developed ways suited to long-term stability. We should respect her patterns in our thoughts, values and deeds.

KEEP THINGS IN PROPORTION
We should choose a human scale for human-made systems. This should allow for access, comprehension, control, creativity and the conviviality of the human community.

BALANCE RIGHTS AND RESPONSIBILITIES
Human rights go hand in hand with a responsibility for our own lives and the fulfilment of obligations towards others, both individually and collectively. Personal excellence is to be encouraged, but not at the expense of others.

DECENTRALIZE AND DEMOCRATIZE
Decision-making should be as local, open and participatory as possible. Power is only to be exercised at a higher level if problems cannot be solved lower down. Democracy and decentralism are important aspects of economic and social justice.

TREAD CAREFULLY
The more complex a situation, the more likely it is that human intervention, especially through technology, will produce unforeseen and undesirable effects.

ALWAYS REMEMBER THAT BAD MEANS PRODUCE BAD ENDS

Good ends can only come about by good means — the 'journey', how we work for change, is inseparable from the destination. In particular, good means require the renunciation of premeditated violence.

Important though each of these principles is, their overall spirit and integration is essential. One-dimensional pursuit of any single principle which contradicts any others could negate the purpose they are all intended to serve.

THE GREEN GOAL

It is sometimes difficult to state simply what Green politics is *for* (as opposed to what it is against). Overall the Green goal is to allow everyone the opportunity to live a fulfilling life, caring for and sharing with each other, future generations and other species, while living sustainably within the capacities of a limited world.

The following chapters seek to explore how governments might begin to move towards this goal, and away from the present slide into ecological and social chaos.

5.
THE POPULATION TIME-BOMB

The explosion in human numbers is the greatest long-term threat to the future of human and non-human inhabitants of the Earth. While nuclear arsenals present grave potential dangers, the predominant crisis of overpopulation is with us today.

When faced with this fact most people bury their heads in the sand. Major political parties and pressure groups in such fields as world poverty share this blinkered approach. Often, books and articles on environmental destruction either simply fail to mention population growth, or go out of their way to deny its dangers. Those who have drawn attention to the problem, like American scientists Paul Ehrlich and Garrett Hardin, have been subject to abuse from across the political spectrum. Robert Malthus, who at the end of the eighteenth century warned of the inherent dangers of rising human numbers, is regularly disinterred for ritual retrial and execution. Could it be that essentially he was right after all, but that too many people have a vested ideological interest in denying the truth?

Human numbers have now passed the five billion mark. They are doubling in shorter and shorter timespans. If trends continue (it is the number of young people in the world that propels the momentum) there will be almost two billion more people within just twenty years. These additional numbers are greater than the total world population of the 1930s. In the time it takes to read this page, about 250 babies will be born. The planet, however, does not grow any bigger.

Some people recognize the danger but hope it will go away by itself, or believe it can be defused by technology, better planning and management or greater affluence. Underlying such optimism is a range of taboos, instincts and values, from religious convictions through concepts of individual rights to plain male machismo. Humans readily apply population control to other species by means of pesticides and herbicides, culling and habitat destruction. We claim it is for their own good as we thin out animals and plants in the name of the environment's capacity to support them. The simple fact is that we humans are no more exempt from biological laws than any other species.

Overpopulation problems in the rest of nature have ways of resolving themselves. Populations which have overshot their environmental limits come crashing down. This would be our eventual fate, though we may try to escape it by directing more of the planet's biological production to our needs. Paul and Anne Ehrlich estimate that 'our one species has co-opted or destroyed some 40 per cent of potential terrestrial productivity'. In so doing, we not only rob other species of their means of life, but we also damage the planet's life-support systems, thus robbing our descendants as well. Nature would eventually solve the problem of human numbers, but in ways unacceptable to civilized thinking. The only alternative, therefore, is human self-restraint.

A BASIC HUMAN RIGHT?

The UN Declaration of Human Rights echoes a widespread belief that there is a socially underwritten right for us to have as many children as we desire. Thus large families are considered to be entitled to the same grants, allowances and general support as small ones. Here, a lethal gap opens between power (to reproduce) and responsibility (to exercise moderation).

American population expert Kingsley Davis has tackled the issue of 'freedom' head-on: 'If having too many children were considered as great a crime against humanity as murder, rape and thievery, we would have no qualms about "taking freedom away". Indeed, it would be defined the other way round: a person having four or more children would be regarded as violating the freedom of those other citizens who must help pay for rearing, educating, and feeding the excess children ... Most "pro-natalists" do not actively want runaway population growth;

they want a solution that leaves them their freedom to have five children if they wish. In short they want a miracle.'

Why do so many people believe in 'miracles' with regard to overpopulation? The urgency of the situation can be blurred by its dynamics. For example, a growth rate of 1 per cent might seem very small but it would double a population's size in a lifetime; the still modest figure of 3 per cent would do the same in just 23 years. Falls in the birthrate can be misleading unless they are compared to the equally important deathrate. A decline in the birthrate could also turn out to be short-lived, and so can give no cause for complacency.

SHORT-SIGHTED SOLUTIONS

The need for direct population policies is clouded by a host of facile answers to the problem of increasing numbers. These include cultivating more land, increasing crop and animal yields, more irrigation, farming the oceans, synthetic foodstuffs and even colonizing the moon and outer space. All create more problems than they solve — soil erosion, deforestation, water pollution, rapid depletion of oil and other scarce resources. Misleadingly they concentrate on one factor: food supply. But in a finite and interconnected world, we increase food production at the expense of other needs. These include vital resources such as living space, energy and water supply, and most importantly, the web of life that maintains the planet's habitability.

Just in terms of food supply, overirrigation, overgrazing, overfishing and overcultivation already reflect the fact that production increases cannot continue. There are worrying signs that we are disrupting climatic patterns to an extent that future food production will suffer. Paul Ehrlich comments, 'the claim that the world can feed eight billion people is the most frequently repeated imbecility of all time'.

Those who play down the problem of overpopulation distort reality in other ways. They cite overproduction in Europe and America to support the myth that poor distribution is the sole problem. Current food surpluses are in fact the product of a system of industrialized farming whose unsustainability and destructiveness have been indicted by such reputable figures as Dr Sicco Mansholt, one of the prime architects of EEC agricultural policy.

In addition, many reassuring figures for world food production are aggregates which conceal unjustifiably optimistic assumptions. Some balance the population/food supply equation by including animal feedstuffs in their calculations of what is currently available for people. Others blame food shortages in regions such as Latin America on unfair land ownership and the use of local farmland to grow cash crops for export.

Desirable though land redistribution and production for local needs are, they do not lessen the need to halt population growth. In the case of El Salvador, for example, it has been estimated that the present rate of increase (3.2 per cent a year) would absorb all the benefits of such reforms in just 21 years. In any case, switching from one crop to another does not significantly lessen the ecological problems attendant on all forms of farming.

People often cite countries such as the Netherlands and Singapore as proof that dense populations can go hand in hand with material prosperity. We should not, however, be thinking merely in terms of density (though this does bring its own serious social problems) but rather the land and resources required, both now and in the future. Such countries can only exist because they prevail upon others to support them. Even regions of comparatively low population densities like the Himalayan foothills can still wreak ecological havoc way beyond their borders, through the pressure they place on the forests of these vital watersheds.

There is the argument that technology can increase the number of people that can be carried by an individual region or by the planet as a whole. At best it can buy time while, in the absence of population policies it fuels further growth in human numbers. This seems to have been the case in Egypt after the construction of the Aswan Dam. The only meaningful measures of what levels of population can be supported are existing, not imagined, social and technological conditions. These suggest that humanity as a whole has already transgressed the planet's carrying capacity.

Some will say they can afford more children. This is confusing economics with ecology. All that they are doing is steering, by their superior purchasing power, the flow of resources in their direction and away from other people and other species.

Others claim that an extra mouth is also an extra pair of hands. This betrays a false understanding of the real wealth of nations. Human endeavour does not create wealth; it can only adapt and transform what it takes from nature's storehouse and the solar energy that replenishes it. No number of 'extra hands' can change the fact that nature cannot keep up with the rising pace of human demands.

IS AFFLUENCE THE ANSWER?

The slow-down in population growth in industrialized nations has taken place at the same time as a general rise in their living standards. It is often assumed, therefore, that global affluence would provide the antidote to rising human numbers. This analogy between the situation in the rich countries and that of today's poor countries is false. The profound social changes that accompanied economic transformation in the developed world have not significantly been repeated in the industrializing countries, where social and cultural traditions still keep birthrates high.

Overpopulation in Europe was masked by emigration to the Americas and the Antipodes (with disastrous impact on those already living there). No New Worlds now offer overspill accommodation. Furthermore, the rate of population growth in Europe and Japan was then slower than that in many industrializing countries today — Mexico, for example, last doubled its population in just twenty years. If we combine statistics for 'crude birthrates' with the age structure of populations in these lands, the prospect is even more serious. Yet many political leaders in rich and poor countries not only campaign against population policies but actually seek to promote further growth. After all, expanding economies demand expanding populations.

The notion that the living standards of the rich countries are attainable by all countries is pure fantasy, as many serious studies of resource availability and the Earth's capacity to absorb pollution demonstrate. Moreover, some of the most rapidly growing populations are in countries like Kenya, where many of the conditions for the supposed demographic slow-down already exist. Development does not always act as a contraceptive, and if poverty does encourage large families, large families conversely often produce poverty.

BLAMING TECHNOLOGY

Another evasion of population problems is to blame 'flawed technologies'. This was popularized by the American socialist and biologist, Barry Commoner. Since the Second World War in particular, human needs have indeed been increasingly met in ways that have heightened waste and ecological damage, for example by the switch to synthetics. However, a return to more natural materials such as wool and cotton would involve such a worsening of overgrazing and harmful monoculture that we would be merely swapping ecological hazards.

Increased personal affluence rather than population growth is sometimes blamed for environmental problems. Although rich countries consume far more resources per person than elsewhere, in the end it is total consumption that matters. A global redistribution of wealth might provide for more people but it would only postpone the day of reckoning. Ultimately redistribution without population control would merely produce universal poverty accompanied by environmental degradation. The central choice in the population debate is this: quantity of human numbers or quality of life?

OVERPOPULATION — EVERYBODY'S BABY

Population pressure is not only a Third World problem. As Paul and Anne Ehrlich say, 'the entire planet is overpopulated'. Countries like Britain and the Netherlands already have too many people. Yet government projections forecast that Britain's population will have grown nearly 4 per cent by the year 2001. Such numbers are a problem in their own right, and are compounding others. How many of these — urban sprawl, unemployment, traffic congestion, homelessness, pressure on welfare services, rural land use conflicts, resource depletion, pollution, destruction of wildlife — would be so severe if there were fewer people?

Garrett Hardin goes to the heart of this issue: 'There is a cliché that says that "freedom is indivisible". Properly interpreted, this saying has some wisdom in it, but there is also a sense in which it is false. Freedom is divisible — and we must find how to divide it if we are to survive in dignity. There are many identifiable freedoms, among which are freedom of speech, freedom of assembly, freedom of association, freedom in the choice of residence, freedom in work, and freedom to travel.

'You can make the list as long as you like. After you have finished, ask yourself this question: Is there one freedom on the list that would increase if our population became twice as great as it is now? Freedom is divisible. If we want to keep the rest of our freedoms, we must restrict the freedom to breed. How we can accomplish this is not at this moment clear; but it is surely subject to rational study. We had better begin our investigations now. We have not long to find acceptable answers.'

In places where growth in human numbers has stabilized, it has done so at levels which are not only overtaxing the environment, but which also make these countries vulnerable to any resurgence. For example, reputable estimates have put Britain's optimum carrying capacity at about 30 million, nearly half its present level of population. In view of this, the urgency of Hardin's message must be emphasized.

CONFRONTING THE ISSUE

There is more to population policy than just birth control. It involves putting together a comprehensive package of technical, economic and social changes to reverse the widespread discrimination in favour of childbearing. The foundation of a population policy must be education. From an early age, children should be taught the constraints placed upon us by the limits of the planet, and their own resulting responsibilities.

In more direct measures a stick and carrot approach is needed, both nationally and internationally. There could be payments for periods of non-pregnancy and non-birth (a kind of no claims bonus); tax benefits for families with fewer than two children; sterilization bonuses; withdrawal of maternity and similar benefits after a second child; larger pensions for people with fewer than two children; free, easily available family planning; more funds for research into means of contraception, especially for men; an end to infertility research and treatment; a more realistic approach to abortion; the banning of surrogate motherhood and similar practices; and the promotion of equal opportunities for women in all areas of life.

Many such measures are already successfully employed in the few places that have confronted the problem of overpopulation. As with other Green policies, they lose their value if pursued in isolation. In such a programme redistribution of wealth, desirable on many other grounds, becomes even more necessary to ensure that parenting does not become a privilege of the rich.

In terms of foreign aid, the cruel truth is that help given to regimes opposed to population policies is counter-productive and should cease. They are the true enemies of life and do not merit support. So too are those religions which do not actively support birth control. Green governments would reluctantly have to challenge head-on such damaging beliefs. To do otherwise would merely exacerbate the problem.

Some measures may seem Draconian. But they are mild compared to what will be required if active steps are not taken now. Moreover, nothing could be more Draconian than that major cultural source of overpopulation, male dominance over women. There is a happy correlation between women's liberation and population control. Doubtless, as ecologist Kenneth Watt says, 'all our problems would be easier to solve if there were fewer people.' Yet this is only one part of a total equation to harmonize the needs of both people and planet.

6.
SUSTAINABLE SUPPLIES

Society has become so insulated within its technological cocoons that it is easy to forget that the resources we draw upon are provided by our environment. No amount of technological sophistication can change that. The production systems of industrial society have become so large and so fast that its thirst for more energy and raw materials has become unsustainable.

The crisis takes two forms. First, there is the squandering of what are properly called the Earth's 'savings': the finite stores of oil, gas, coal and minerals. Second, and more worrying, is the rapid erosion of our 'income': those resources drawn from sunlight, soil and water which ecological cycles are increasingly unable to replenish, such is the assault by humanity on them.

In a mere blink on the timescale of human evolution, industrial society has been depleting and impairing Earth's 'supply system' at a phenomenal rate. It treats the Earth like some enormous warehouse, a lifeless horn of plenty there to satisfy our whims. Rising human numbers, greater levels of personal consumption and more powerful technologies create a demand, for which supplies are diminishing. The prospect is one of inevitable haemorrhage in the lifeblood of industrialism — the cheap and ready flow of abundant energy and minerals. Americans, for example, have used more minerals and fossil fuels during the past half-century than all the other peoples of the world throughout human history. To spread such consumption levels to the rest of the world's exploding numbers would require over 130 times the world output of 1979. Attempting such a feat would soon bankrupt the Earth.

If it were just a problem of our factories running short of, say, nickel or tungsten, the barrier might not be insurmountable. In the past humanity has been able to switch from one resource base to another, even though individual communities have sometimes paid a grievous price. What has changed is the sheer scale of our dependence on so many resources: fossil fuels, sand, gravel and stone, water, metals, animal and plant products, wood, fertilizer, plastics, rubber, synthetic fibres ... the list seems endless. Each item is obtained at the expense of other resources — it takes energy to get energy supplies — and at the cost of human and environmental damage, at every stage from exploration and extraction, through processing to use and the discarding of the 'waste'.

Industrialism will increasingly have to feed itself from sources of poorer grade and in more remote locations. The ground subsidence, the waste tips, the oil spills and blow-outs, the water pollution, the health hazards, the boom-time inflation and the ghost towns associated with old minefields and oil wells will be visited upon green fields and pastures new. The short-term cost is likely to be partly economic — inflation due to rising resource costs — and partly political. More communities will be forced to have on their doorsteps open-cast sites, mines and wells they do not want.

Even more dangerous is that many resources only occur in a few locations. The leading industrial countries protect their stakes by military means — the French in Central Africa, the Americans in the Middle East, the British in the South Atlantic. The risk of 'resource wars' is plain to see. The battleground may turn out not to be a particular oil field or mine, but rivers such as the Nile, Euphrates and Mekong.

Already the smash, grab and run cycle seems set to be repeated on the last untouched part of the planet — Antarctica. The potential consequences for the ecological cycles which depend on this mass of frozen water are incalculable, and will not be known until it is too late. In the long run paying the price solves nothing. We will only be further down a blind alley from which future generations will find it almost impossible to escape.

What about the 'lifeblood' of humans themselves — food and water? Again, all the signs suggest that we are taking too much too fast. High levels of agricultural output depend on increased inputs, with harmful side effects which put the total resource balance into the red. There is ample evidence of declining productivity across world croplands, ranges, forests and fisheries. In the next ten years it is estimated we will lose 275 billion tons of topsoil, around 8 per cent of the already depleted total of that most fundamental of all resources. Innovation in farming and medicine is being irreversibly undermined as we lose the genetic resources of plants and animals driven into extinction.

The concept of scarcity is fundamental, if we are to understand how to find the resources for our future society. It is rooted in the biophysical realities of a finite planet, ruled and limited by entropy and ecology. The spectacle of farmers being paid to plough their crops into the ground, of idle industrial plant or falling petrol prices can mislead, since they tempt us to see the problem as one of human restrictions on production which only have to be released to usher in a world of material abundance.

ALCHEMY UNLIMITED

Many economists believe that higher prices will solve the problem by generating more supplies from sources which were previously uneconomical to tap. Yet this is no answer for those who cannot afford to pay, and anyway, the resources remain finite. There are certainly massive amounts of minerals in the Earth's crust but extracting them would create overwhelming amounts of rock waste as well as disrupting and poisoning water systems. Worse, it would demand even greater energy resources, which themselves are limited in supply, and result in more pollution and harmful climatic change. And no amount of price rise can conjure back to life what has gone for good, be it an exhausted mine or an extinct species.

Other people look to recycling. The laws of thermodynamics tell us that the use of energy is a one-way process. You cannot relight a fire from yesterday's ashes, nor can a car run on exhaust fumes. Material recovery, while promising, cannot overcome the need to reduce and stabilize consumption.

These laws apply to matter as much as to energy. At every stage in the use of a raw material some of it is lost for ever. Recovering the rest and restoring it to a resuable form requires energy and creates pollution. The situation is made worse by the complexity of many modern products and the physical area over which they are scattered in terms of both production and consumption. Making things last longer would, of course, help greatly. Planned obsolescence and designs that thwart attempts at repair and renewal are obvious enemies of a conserver society.

SWITCHING TRACKS

Dreamers of cornucopian plenty have one last trick up their sleeve. The technological wizard will wave a magic wand and provide society with replacement resources. These will substitute for those whose financial cost, or health and environmental impact, can no longer be borne.

But substitution merely locks us into a deadly game of musical chairs. The next century may well see humanity running into a series of resource shortages for which substitutes would need to be devised at an unprecedented rate. Some materials have irreplaceable qualities. For others the substitutes are likely to be inferior in performance, more costly, more polluting, or may themselves depend on further scarce resources. Plastics provide an obvious example, but 'alternative' technologies can also demand rare and hazardous chemicals, as is the case with some solar cells.

The greatest hopes of the cornucopians, however, are placed upon new technologies. Like the cavalry in an old movie riding to the last-minute rescue, the microprocessor, nuclear fusion and biotechnology are being heralded as our salvation. Each has its own problems, which are outlined later. All remain bound by the basic laws of energy and matter. At best they purchase a breathing space. If social values — especially the equation of progress with increasing consumption — remain unchanged, technologies such as the silicon chip can make matters worse. Their very speed allows the wheels of production to spin faster, soaking up even more resources.

SUSTAINING EXPLOITATION ... INTEGRATING OPPRESSION

Fears over future resource supplies are not confined to Green circles. The word 'sustainability' appears in one official report after another. Yet it begs more questions than it answers. Some of its roots can be traced back to the wasteful destruction of America's forests at the turn of the century, in response to which came calls for the 'scientific management' of resources and the practice of what was called 'sustained yield'.

Conservation was equated with efficiency. As a result, old woods were replaced by uniform 'tree factories' in which toxic spraying threatened wildlife and humans alike. This reflects what has been called the ideology of 'resourcism', preparing the way for yet further manipulation and exploitation. 'Resourcism' justifies the assault upon anything, social or environmental, that is considered to lack 'utility' or to stand in the way of productivity.

You can find the same attitude in books from supposedly environmentalist organizations. Known reserves of particular resources are totted up. Colourful symbols locate further sources. In reality, these places are often the lands of tribal peoples, of wildlife habitats and of thriving farming communities. The inconvenient fact that they would be destroyed if such resources were to be exploited is glossed over.

There is also much talk about 'integration'. The worthy goal is a multiple use of resources, especially land. But the central issues remain: what kind of use, for whose benefit, and at what level? Interest in the environment may receive greater recognition than before, but in conventional planning the environment and non-human species remain factors on a list of many interests, to be traded away if political expediency, price fluctuations, or 'cost/benefit' analysis should deem it necessary. Furthermore, integrating bad practices in farming, forestry and tourism compound the problem. True integration puts one requirement first and foremost — the continuity of healthy environments and their associated lifeforms. It is around this that we can then integrate everything else.

Only such a holistic perspective points the way forward in the problem of resources. We need to think in terms of the sustainable and balanced satisfaction of all kinds of human need — material, psychological and spiritual. We should not try to realize the aspirations of one community, culture or generation by sacrificing another. We should not strive to fulfil human wants by destroying other species. Only within this framework can we find lasting ways of supplying the needs of a truly worthwhile society.

TOWARDS A CONSERVER SOCIETY

The central task is fourfold:
- A reduction in the total amount of the resources we are consuming.
- A switch from non-renewable to renewable sources.
- The use of resources as close as possible to their natural form, to minimize 'entropy' overheads.
- Using of local resources, where possible, for local needs.

By these means, production and consumption would be brought into equilibrium with what the environment can provide indefinitely. Different terms have been used to describe this balance such as 'steady-state economics' or 'the materials/energy balance principle', but the essential purpose is the same.

USE LESS

Reducing the throughput of energy and materials depends on a combination of factors. First, the only long-term way to reduce consumption is to stabilize and then reduce the number of consumers. The best resources policies are doomed to failure if not linked to population policy. Next, we must change our life-styles to reflect values of 'enough' instead of 'more', and of quality instead of quantity. Then we must dismantle the economic structures and means of production which cause excessive use of resources, and create waste. This would require an increase in production efficiency, and in the life of the product through better quality and design, thus permitting maximum re-use, repair and, ultimately, recycling. Finally we must find peaceful ways of resolving our differences. Wartime destruction and the resources devoured by insatiable military programmes will cancel out everything we may otherwise achieve.

RENEW MORE

We cannot easily switch from non-renewable to renewable resources. We are currently as dependent on oil as heroin addicts on their drug. The by-products of oil are used at home, at work, at play, and especially in forms of transport. What we can do, however, is to discourage the use of finite and diminishing resources in all fields except where no alternatives are possible. As far as is practicable, resources which are more abundant should be used to buy time during the transition to technologies that harness renewable solar energy, biological resources and the changed living patterns to go with them.

KEEP CLOSE TO SOURCE

The third task is to minimize energy conversions and material processing. A wholefood diet and passive solar heating are good examples. Finally, a conserver society requires a greater emphasis on local and regional self-reliance. Until recently 'vernacular' architecture used mainly indigenous materials, avoiding wasteful transport and creating buildings of a variety and beauty that many contemporaries would envy.

SOME PRACTICAL SUGGESTIONS

Green policies for conservation and equilibrium vary from the general to those that concern specific resources; here we are concerned with the broad direction of policy. Taxing, true cost pricing, subsidies, regulations and public information together form the overall programme.

The first steps of any Green government would be to review existing grants, tax allowances and other ways in which investment patterns are influenced. Those that undermine resource conservation — unnecessary 'improvements', the premature writing-off of equipment, or refurbishments to save tax — would immediately be ended. In the short term conventional government tools would have to be used. This would mean higher rates of value-added tax on resource-intensive products and correspondingly lower ones on activities that are labour-intensive, thus encouraging re-use and repair. Discounts for large users, especially of energy, would be stopped, while subsidies for energy conservation and recycling would be increased. Greens would encourage labour-intensive institutions and technologies rather than those that demand high physical and financial capital. Green economic policy would end measures which penalize the employment of people and encourage mechanization. In general, the burden of taxation would be shifted onto resource use.

Performance standards, and an end to commercial secrecy about the projected lifespans of goods and components, would encourage quality and durability in products. Processes and products which frustrate re-use and repair would be penalized. Producers would be obliged to make available necessary spare parts and instructions for the repair of their products.

Recycling would also play its part. Local authority and commercial waste disposal enterprises would have to provide the means for collecting recyclable materials separated at source, with lower charges for the customers of such a service. A necessary aspect of the programme would be to contain pollutants that contaminate otherwise recyclable materials, such as water and sewage. Green policy would deliberately make virgin resources comparatively more expensive, as an incentive to reuse, repair, recycling and the careful management of the choice of resources used in products.

Upper limits for national consumption of the critical raw materials — oil, gas, and certain minerals — would have to be established. There would be an immediate general freeze at current levels, followed by a progressive reduction of the rates of consumption. A stimulating suggestion of how this could be achieved is provided by economist Herman Daly, with his idea of an annual public auction of the right to supply limited quantities of resources. Foreign imports would be subject to a similar quota system. Maximum limits would be set on sales to individual enterprises to avoid an over-concentration of economic power in too few hands. Unused raw materials would, after a fixed time, have to be sold back to the government at the original price.

Through quotas, the use of renewable resources could be contained safely within rates of natural replenishment. Overpowerful technologies shown to threaten the regenerative capacity of fisheries, fields or forests would be banned.

A department of resource conservation and planning would be a necessary agency to look after the measures that require government action. It would, for example, plan how much of a particular mineral was needed in a given year, while a ministry of land use would determine the best sites for extraction. The ministries of environment protection and of health would ensure this was done in ways which had the least impact on place and people.

7.
THE BIG CLEAN-UP

Society not only 'imports' resources from the environment; it also 'exports' wastes and pollution back to it. The overconsumption and resource depletion by our industrial society is everywhere paralleled by greater pollution. Contrary to those who view pollution simply as a sign of bad resource management, the Green view is that its roots lie in the very laws of energy and matter. Their transformation by the human economy inevitably generates by-products which return as pollutants to the environmental 'sink' of air, soil and sea.

THE STORY OF POLLUTION

There is nothing new about pollution — some say that the ancient Romans were victims of lead poisoning from their drinking vessels, while the expression 'mad as a hatter' recalls the hazards of some traditional craft trades. Modern society, however, has dramatically speeded up the process.

Part of the problem is the sheer volume of pollution. This reflects both the scale of production and its concentration in specific locations. The impact of farming, quarrying, processing and manufacture interrupts natural cycles, perverting the flow of energy and materials through the environment. The radiation hazards of what comes out of nuclear reactors, for example, are far worse than the hazards associated with what goes into them. The Minimata mercury poisonings in Japan, the scourge of asbestosis, nitrate pollution of drinking water and threats from cadmium and lead all spotlight the price of such intervention. It is a price also being paid by the rest of the environment. A typical example is the dramatic speeding up of the rate at which lakes 'age' when artificial additions of phosphorus and nitrogen from fertilizers and detergents cause over-abundant growth.

Natural systems can break down and recycle biodegradable wastes providing we keep them within limits of tolerance. Over-population and overconsumption, however, are swamping nature's ability to do so. The problem of quantity has been compounded by a revolution in the kinds of materials needed to satisfy human wants. From plastics to plutonium, we have created materials of which nature has no evolutionary experience (they are not simply another set of 'chemicals'). Their dangers have been highlighted by accidents at manufacturing plants such as Seveso in Italy and Bhopal in India, or by tanker disasters at sea. More dangerous though less spectacular is the insidious effect of their everyday use.

There is ample evidence of the hazards of synthetic substances such as DDT, dioxin and PCBs on living systems. These are but the tip of a chemical time bomb. A recent count in the Great Lakes of North America identified 460 toxic chemicals, literally from A (Aldrin) to Z (Zytron). Many are unknown to the public — until the media break the news of their sudden withdrawal because of their dangers. The deaths of birds such as eagles and pelicans, at the top of the local food chains, is a warning bell for all species.

It is easy to worry about the wrong things. We may get angry about farm smells, litter in the street and broken bottles on the beach. Though nuisances, these are the least of our problems. As parents we worry about the danger to our children's health from leaded petrol in cars. But far graver, long-term hazards come from pollution, causing wholesale environmental degradation and climatic disruption. The chemical cocktail known as acid rain assaults lakes, forests and soils, threatening a long-term erosion of the biological productivity of resources that we cannot do without. The protective ozone layer in the sky is likewise under threat, not just from chlorofluorocarbons (CFCs) but from a whole host of artificial additions to the atmosphere.

Last but certainly not least is the risk to the planet's heat balance caused by human activity, particularly from the burning of fossil fuels and the consequent release of carbon dioxide. This trend is made worse by what we are taking out of the environment; deforestation removes the life forms which help absorb the carbon dioxide during photosynthesis. Slowly but surely adding to this heating up of the planet is thermal pollution itself, the unavoidable by-product of every conversion of energy.

One of the worst changes that industrialism has made to pollution is not the addition of individual new pollutants, but their combined effects. Acid rain and the photochemical smog above many modern cities are examples of what is known as synergy. Some half a million chemicals are in common use; about another thousand are added each year. Yet we know next to nothing about their interaction and combined effects, and the scale of the problem suggests that we never will.

We are treating the Earth as a living laboratory and ourselves as the chief guinea pigs. Artificial additions to natural background radiation are perhaps the greatest 'experiment' of all. Yet any danger to the public is vigorously denied, small comfort for the victims of thalidomide, of Minimata, of Agent Orange in Vietnam and the A-bomb tests in Australia and the Pacific.

In his book *Cover-Up* Nicholas Hildyard has documented just how systematically business and government set about concealing the risks to which the public is being subjected. When individuals do unmask the dangers, they often become the objects of vicious witch-hunts such as happened to Rachel Carson, author of the famed *Silent Spring*; in the case of Karen Silkwood it appears to have led to murder.

FALSE REASSURANCES

Governments and officials contribute to playing down the pollution problem. In Britain, the Conservative government has consistently demanded conclusive evidence before taking even minimal action. Business has resisted change; the removal of lead from petrol was 'impossible' or 'unnecessary'. Scientists study pollutants in isolation and debate endlessly whether tree deaths are the result of a pest, a disease, or some specific type or source of pollutant.

The problem might be better answered by turning the question round; why is nature losing its resistance and resilience? This would point us to the real issue: the total effect on living systems of industrial pollution, which is undermining them one after another.

Eugene Schwartz pinpoints the flaw in claims that new substances, or additional use of existing ones, are safe: 'Science and technology can provide no values to choose and guide the development of more science and technology, nor can scientists define safe limits for any of the negative aspects of technology such as radiation or pollution levels. The establishment of any limits affecting humans are not discoverable *a priori* for, according to the axioms of science, these limits can only be derived from observation and measurement. In a sense, technological civilization is an experiment to test the "limits of the earth".'

The dangers can be overlooked by even the most diligent researcher, let alone those with a vested interest in the *status quo*. Many pollutants are difficult to detect, and monitoring is often inadequate. We do not know who has been exposed to what for how long. The real culprit of a disease or death may be masked by a more immediate factor. Medical diagnoses are not always accurate; people have often left their work or moved house. Effects may take very long periods to show up; symptoms of risk may not be spotted in small samples. Our attention is grabbed by major accidents rather than slow attrition.

For many forms of pollution there may well be threshold levels below which they are safe. But we cannot tell in advance what these are and when they will be transgressed. In a field like radiation exposure, every advance in our understanding has led to calls for substantial revisions downwards from levels previously believed to be safe. The evidence here and elsewhere suggests that humans should play safe and err on the side of maximum caution. In particular we should stop talking about 'average' levels and 'average' people. As Edward Goldsmith comments, 'if our government were really concerned about the effect of pollutants, it is not the critical groups of today that it would cater for, but all the possible critical groups of an unpredictable tomorrow. This means that we should not be catering for Mr Average but for Mr Maximum'. In reality the industrial growth society sets permissible levels of pollution which are what its farming, forestry, mining and manufacture can cope with economically, not what is reliably safe for either people or the environment.

Pollution does not go away of its own accord. The conventional answers are failing. The policy of shifting wastes around or of concentrating them, in the hope that they will thereby become safer or more manageable, has proved far from safe. While incidents such as the Aberfan coal-tip disaster catch our attention, greater hazards lie in the slow leaching from the thousands of toxic chemical dumps (now joined by radioactive waste sites) dotted about the land.

The other conventional solution is dilution. People have great faith that the sheer size of the atmosphere and the oceans will dilute the pollutants we dump there, until they become harmless. In fact biological magnification works in reverse order. Poisons are progressively concentrated as they move through food chains — heading straight back in our direction.

PUTTING A PRICE ON POLLUTION

An increasingly popular policy is that 'the polluter must pay'. This might seem a reasonable response to those enterprises, private or nationalized, which boost their profits by avoiding the full costs of the pollution they cause. The costs are passed on to the general public and the environment at large, for it is here that the bill is finally picked up. A Green government would try to make the price that firms charge for their products reflect more accurately the true costs of their production.

However, there are serious limitations to this approach. Many forms of pollution are a combination of substances from diverse sources. Moreover, the contribution from an individual enterprise or household is often negligible; the damage arises out of cumulative additions. It would be impossible to calculate fairly who should pay what costs. And, critically, some consequences of pollution are irrevocable, and no amount of taxes can make amends even if we could put a price on what has been lost. So fines and other punishments are of limited application. They embody misleading notions about the pollution problem, not least that there is such a thing as 'optimal pollution'. This fiscal approach is also flawed (like its technological cousin discussed below) by a false perception of pollution, seeing it merely as a failure to make use of waste by-products which, by a few pulls on the right lever, could be turned into new forms of wealth.

TECHNOLOGY TO THE RESCUE?

Another conventional remedy is to use various gadgets to clean up polluting processes. Some forms of pollution, however, cannot be avoided, and are too large-scale and dispersed to be controlled by such means. Examples include waste heat, carbon dioxide release and fertilizer run-off. Others are too small. It is the tiniest of particles that are often the most dangerous, and they are the most difficult to contain. Technological gadgets merely shift the problem around, often at the expense of more energy and material inputs and therefore more pollution. Favourite devices such as refuse incineration, sulphur extractors in power stations and catalytic converters in cars cost money and energy while at the same time generating new pollutants.

There is no such thing as zero emission, and attempts

progressively to reduce levels of pollution normally trigger off an explosive growth in the financial cost. Yet for some pollutants, especially deadly plutonium, nothing less than 100 per cent containment will do. Successes can sometimes be achieved by better controls and management, but these are quickly cancelled out if, in so doing, we produce and consume more energy and materials.

What about the dangers of accidental pollution? We hear about 'fail-safe' designs and procedures; for the 'fail safe' to be true, there must be flawless design and construction, no malfunctions, no operating errors and perfect protection from acts of God and acts of people. This might be conceivable in a make-believe world, but bears little relation to reality as newspaper headlines about the Torrey Canyon, Seveso, Bhopal, Amoco Cadiz, Chernobyl, assorted dam failures, 'plane crashes and many more disasters all attest.

GREEN POLLUTION POLICY

The only way to stop these assaults on ourselves and our environment is to generate less pollution. Since so much pollution is inevitable, given the passage of energy and materials through the economy, we will only reduce it by lowering the quantities of resources we use. Schemes for depletion quotas, and raw material taxes on energy and other resources, are the best way to do this. In some circumstances, such as the use of nitrogen fertilizers, limits would have to be set by physical quotas.

The only long-term answer is to reduce overall economic activity, introduce policies for population control and promote less damaging technologies. Some forms of pollution are, however, so toxic in quality (some heavy metals, for example) or so devastating in impact (such as chlorofluorocarbons on the ozone layer) that they require direct regulations on their use and disposal, enforced by independent and well-staffed agencies.

The list of substances and processes deserving an immediate ban, such as DDT, the open incineration of hazardous chemicals, non-biodegradable plastic packaging, phosphate-containing detergents, would fill many pages of this book. A number of them have been or are about to be banned in some parts of the world. Recent measures in California (the Safe Drinking Water and Toxic Enforcement Act) to force manufacturers to make public the chemicals they use is an example to be followed and expanded. In the case of nuclear facilities, the only answer is to ban the entire industry.

For all their limitations, many recycling programmes are

worthy of encouragement, both to conserve resources and to limit pollution. So too are some 'technofixes' such as fluidized-bed combustion as a measure against air pollution.

A particular focus on pollution issues should be the workplace, where progress over occupational health and safety would pay dividends for workers, the general public and the environment. Three rights are important — the right to know relevant information, the right to participate in proper consultation and negotiation, and the right to refuse to work in hazardous conditions. The breaking of health and safety regulations in the workplace and anti-pollution laws outside must be treated as crimes against society, which outrank many other offences now punished by harsh fines and imprisonment. Recent cases in the USA, in which criminal charges relating to pollution incidents have been brought against individuals within companies, point one way forward. Though government agencies could and should bring such actions, individuals and groups must be similarly empowered to challenge activities which threaten either themselves or society as a whole.

Decisions about many aspects of pollution are made under conditions of inevitable ignorance, but guidance is available from nature herself. As biologist Barry Commoner notes, 'the consistent absence of a chemical constituent from natural biological systems is an extraordinarily meaningful fact'. We must always proceed with the utmost caution. In fact, 'the slightest probability of a pollutant's guilt must be sufficient reason to warrant its removal from the market' (Edward Goldsmith). Designs and operating procedures must be judged not on claims of being fail-safe, but on their tolerance of failure. In other words, we must accept that things may go wrong and ensure that the consequences are not socially and environmentally unacceptable. Only if we begin to initiate all these measures seriously will nature's own self-cleansing mechanisms eventually be able to restore pure air, clean oceans and sweet water.

8.
PROTECTING
THE WEB

Society depends on the environment for all the resources it consumes. But there is also a vast range of 'free services' through which nature maintains the habitability of the Earth. The difficulties of keeping astronauts alive in space demonstrates how vital are the life-support functions performed by natural ecological systems.

Unlike industrial society, nature has no energy problem. The process of photosynthesis harnesses only a tiny fraction of incoming solar energy. Yet from less than 5 per cent of what it receives, nature has produced wonderful diversity and richness: more than quarter of a million species of plants and well over a million species of animals. If we humans could learn to do so much from so little, we might have fewer social and ecological problems.

Through evolution, nature has produced a virtual infinity of working, flexible compromises to sustain, repair and regulate itself. It is a system well able to cope with change. Where volcanoes explode, nature soon heals the wounds with new vegetation. The Amazonian jungles have sustained their luxuriance for countless centuries. The Earth seems to have created and maintained optimum conditions for the flourishing of life.

But there is one change which nature cannot seem to accommodate — technological human society.

All other plants and animals work together in self-maintaining ecosystems, fitting into the biosphere as a whole. First with agriculture, now with the industrialization of one part of the Earth after the other, humanity is breaking apart the web of life. When Greens talk of an unbalancing of nature, we are not thinking of the loss of some fixed 'Garden of Eden'; the issue is the growing impairment and loss of resilience of the planet's life-support mechanisms.

FREE SERVICE

The dangers become clear once we understand fully how much we depend on what the Ehrlichs call 'natural life-support services'. We humans may well be exceptional in some ways. Nevertheless, like all species we will suffer if the ecological interactions between life forms and physical environments are undermined. Together, these 'ecoservices' can — if undamaged — provide an optimum human environment. After careful study of the evidence Drs Iltis, Loucks and Andrews concluded: 'Unique as we may think we are, it seems likely that we are genetically programmed to a natural habitat of clean air and a varied green landscape, just like any other mammal.'

We benefit from countless resources, such as foodstuffs, medicine, natural insecticides, clothing materials, wood, biomass fuels, oils, rubber and glues. The interaction between the immense herds of buffalo and once flourishing plant communities provided native Americans with more 'meat on the hoof' than there is today on the plains of the Prairies. Many further examples of resources lost or reduced by the disruption of ecological processes have been documented by the Ehrlichs in their book *Extinction*.

Also vital to a habitable planet are indirect services including the maintenance of atmospheric balances; air purification; amelioration of the weather; provision of shelter; advance warning of pollution problems; regulation of the water cycle; disposal of wastes and recycling of nutrients; generation and maintenance of soil fertility; pest and disease control; pollination; maintenance of the 'library' of genetic information vital for new medicines, foodstuffs and other needs; and pleasure, inspiration and inner renewal derived from human contact with unmodified nature.

Particularly damaging is the destruction of forests and wetlands, each a prime 'life-support' system. Forests act as buffers against excess carbon dioxide in the atmosphere and stabilize the climate; they enhance rainfall; they protect soil and act as sponges against an excess downhill flow of water; they purify and cool the air; they absorb noise; they provide habitats for an incredible variety of wildlife; they convert solar energy into a host of resources, of which lumber is just one; and they are beautiful. The further we move from natural, diverse forests to single-species, even-age plantations, the more these priceless and irreplaceable 'life-support' functions are lost.

Contrary to popular belief wetlands are not wastelands. They are vital to the global cycles of carbon, nitrogen and other key elements. Locally, they act as water storage reservoirs; purification areas for waste water and biodegradable effluents; breeding places and nurseries for fish; sources of shellfish; and protection against storm floods. As Dieren and Hummelinck note, estuaries do the work of several thousand purification plants — for free.

A HOME IN PERFECT ORDER

These 'ecoservices' cannot be replaced by human technology. Technological substitutes are either non-existent or hugely expensive. As Ehrenfeld comments, 'our most glittering improvements over nature are too often a fool's solution to a problem that has been isolated from context, a transient, local maximization that is bound to be followed by mostly undesirable counter-adjustments throughout the system'. We sometimes behave like do-it-yourself fanatics trying to 'do up' what is perfectly decorated and in perfect repair, and the boomerang effects can be sudden and dramatic. Human attempts to improve upon the 'ecoservices' provided by the river Nile by building the Aswan Dam have met with disastrous consequences. Western-style farming and the replacement of natural woodlands by tree farms create longer-term instabilities, dependent on the repair kits of fertilizers and pesticides with their own attendant problems.

Human intervention can have less direct repercussions. Warfare against the tsetse fly in Africa (financed by organizations such as the EEC) might seem a sensible 'home improvement'. Yet this 'pest' protected vulnerable lands from the overgrazing that swiftly followed its eradication.

There are countless examples of the dangers of working against rather than with nature's ways. William Ophuls has compared nature to a well-made watch: 'If one pokes at this arrangement carelessly, there is a strong likelihood that it will suffer damage.' Species extinctions, spreading deserts, dying forests and lakes are all signs that the size of the human population and the power of its technology are now causing damage that is irreparable on a human timescale. Nature may well be able to do without us, but we cannot do without it.

Given this perspective, debates about when a particular resource might run out can miss the real point. It is the damaging side-effects on the 'ecoservices' from increased use of energy and material resources that is the most fundamental 'limit to growth', not the availability of the resources themselves.

THE DESTRUCTION OF DIVERSITY

We have a crisis of social, biological and ecological uniformity. It spreads every time we unravel the web of life by putting more land under the plough; by grazing herds of domesticated animals; by planting tree farms; by drowning land under reservoirs and tidal barrages; by burying it under tarmac and concrete; by digging and mining; by reseeding moorlands; by channelling waterways; by draining marshes or filling in estuaries; and by many more interventions to meet the rising demands of a rising population. Sometimes it is on a large scale, such as the destruction of rainforests to make way for cattle ranches and mines. More often, it is the accumulation of countless otherwise insignificant actions, of every new housing estate or motorway.

The scale of the destruction is awesome and its speed is growing. In Britain, some 40 per cent of the country's remaining semi-natural woodlands have been cleared or converted to plantations since 1945. Tree cover may have increased dramatically, but nearly all of it takes the form of exotic conifers in regimented boxes. Over 50 per cent of marshes, and 30 per cent of upland grassland, heath and blanket bog have gone. The toll includes human-made but species-rich habitats such as hedgerows (25 per cent gone), hay meadows (95 per cent gone) and chalk grassland (80 per cent gone). Areas from the New Forest to the flow country of Caithness and Sutherland are at risk from 'development'. Even protected areas are not safe: every year 4 per cent of sites of scientific interest are severely destroyed, mainly by agricultural development.

DOWN THE PLUGHOLE

Some would dismiss current losses of plants and animals by pointing to the frequency of ice ages. In the past creatures such as the dinosaurs became extinct and, so the argument goes, there is nothing new about what is happening today. Perhaps we are living in a temporary warm period whose ending will doom many species anyway. The historical point is, however, not the fate of any particular species, but the fact that during an ice age life as a whole went on. Small mammals were ready to take over from the dinosaurs, while dinosaurs bequeathed much of their genetic endowment to birds and reptiles.

The Ehrlichs spotlight two key biological processes — speciation and extinction: 'It is as if speciation were a tap running new species into a sink and extinction were a drain. Humanity has become a major agent of extinction, opening the drain ever wider ... at the same time inhibiting the compensating process, speciation.' As a result, species are now disappearing far more rapidly than they are appearing. We are talking both of whole species and, as importantly, of variety within them.

Surely we should be trying to heal our ailing environment, rather than pondering the meaning of ice ages. The loss of individual species may not directly affect humans, nor necessarily disrupt regional or global ecology. But what matters is their right to exist, and our responsibility, as thinking animals, to respect that right.

LIMITS OF ENVIRONMENTAL PROTECTION

Concern about environmental destruction has grown rapidly since the turn of the century. It has led to the creation of various types of park and reserve and, in some countries, quite elaborate systems of planning.

Many public and private organizations, including some of the biggest multinational corporations, now have staffs with an environmental brief, and they donate generously to environmentally worthwhile causes. Advertising employs more and more words and images reflecting environmental awareness. There has been major growth of non-governmental organizations and pressure groups. Much time, money and effort is spent acquiring land, lobbying in the corridors of political and economic power, sitting on committees, producing reports, and generally waving the flag of environmental protection. The main political parties all make noises about the environment, an issue rarely aired before.

The roots of mainstream environmentalism contain inbuilt contradictions. The most dominant influence is what has been called the 'gospel of efficiency', and this was particularly evident in the American conservation movement early this century. The movement opposed the waste of resources, and saw conservation as a tool for further expansion. Its commitment was to squeezing as much as possible out of nature, albeit in less immediately damaging ways.

This kind of conservation is now an industry in its own right, with its own experts. It is possible to obtain 'operating manuals for spaceship earth' (Buckminster Fuller), atlases of planetary management and whole earth catalogues as if the planet were some giant superstore. The approach of official — sometimes even unofficial — conservation is too often about management, planning and better technologies, cultivating value-free 'objectivity' and compartmentalizing issues in the same way as other areas of modern intellectual life. The Norwegian writer Johann Galtung has suggested the term 'ecocrat' to describe this sort of conservationist. Many spend so much time trying to get a better deal within the system that they cannot see beyond it. They become bound up with the preservation of the *status quo*.

Often official environmentalism is only able to make belated attempts to mitigate the worst side-effects of what is accepted as 'inevitable' (more roads, more hotels, more dams, more factory estates, more suburbs). This should not lead us to doubt the commitment and value of many individuals in these bodies. Much of their difficulty lies in the totally inadequate scale of their resources. As a result they are unable to press the vitally important questions of values, motives and long-term goals. They avoid asking why so much environmental destruction is taking place.

The official approach to conservation can be compared to the little Dutch boy, with his finger in the dyke. Holes are appearing all over the dam wall, and only a lessening of the pressures causing those cracks can succeed in stemming the flood. We can't solve our problems just by trying to guide the floodwater away from sensitive spots.

There is even talk of acceptable losses and of the need to concentrate on those species that experts judge worth preserving. This is strategically wrong, for the complex interactions between species and habitats make simple classifications like useful/not useful or savable/unsavable meaningless. It is also tactically wrong to announce a willingness to accept a lower price in advance of negotiations. Nothing is solved by the token preservation of a few habitats and a few species, to appease our conscience.

In the name of 'realism' or in order to win friends in high places, some conservationists pull their punches, restricting their demands to calls for more research information. If we wait for all the facts, no action will ever be taken in time. What is needed is not environmental cosmetics, but a recognition of the comprehensive threat and the need for a comprehensive response. In cosmic terms, the whole of planet Earth needs protection.

DEVELOPMENT IS DESTRUCTION

The threat to natural diversity is directly linked to population pressures. Meeting the needs of growing human numbers inevitably means more ecological simplification. While we rightly worry about industrial pollution, there are deeper problems in the extent and intensity of human-made production systems for obtaining the foodstuffs, fibres and materials for shelter that we all need.

Here we work directly against ecological stability: nature, left to her own devices, does not create fields full of lettuces nor forests full of single-age fir trees. This is the Achilles' heel of human civilization. We can cut back on the dream of each family owning four TV sets, three cars, two houses, and one yacht. But we cannot live without the basics of life. Still further increases in the production of food and other essentials, as envisaged by the apostles of world 'development', will only bring a greater undermining of the 'ecoservices' we all need to survive. Human production systems such as farms and timber plantations are intrinsically unstable compared to the natural systems they replace. Annual cropping and the cultivation of uniform species inevitably creates ecological problems like soil erosion, pests and diseases.

DEFENDING DIVERSITY

The answer to ecosimplification is not easy. Like all species, humans draw upon environments to satisfy their needs. This must be done in ways as compatible as possible with the patterns of diversity and succession found in nature.

Part of the solution will be a move away from industrialized farming and forestry based on artificial fertilizers, pesticides and heavy mechanization. The framework of subsidies and quotas must be altered to encourage a shift to self-sustaining and less damaging forms of organic agriculture. Groups such as the Soil Association have demonstrated that we can produce food not only of sufficient quantity but also of superior taste and nutritional quality with far fewer damaging side-effects and less dependence on the availability of cheap oil. The opportunity of current surpluses in countries like Britain should not be used to set aside land for golf courses and conifer plantations while leaving the rest more intensively cultivated than ever. Instead it is an opportunity to reduce the intensity of all farming.

Traditional practices such as coppicing similarly permit production while remaining compatible with healthy and diverse woodlands. The culling of wild herds is at least less damaging than their replacement by domesticated animals.

The right to treat land as private property for whatever purposes its owner decides is incompatible with long-term environmental protection and social justice. Planning controls and penalties should be used to limit environmental degradation. The countryside would be brought within a comprehensive planning system based on the ecologically appropriate use of different kinds of environments. On our coastlines no more marinas, fish farms nor tidal barrages would be permitted. Undeveloped stretches of shorelines, of riverside corridors and of marshland would also be kept free from encroachment. Surviving deciduous woodlands and hedgerow trees would be given full statutory protection against clearance.

In the short term, these and other measures, such as stopping any further encroachment into existing green belts, are needed to buy time. At present the controls are insufficient and can encourage developers to keep coming back with their proposals, making minor modifications until they finally get their way.

On existing farmlands and forestry plantations there are some admirable schemes to restore spaces for wildlife. Recreating an individual pond or copse might not seem very significant, yet it all adds up, especially if society is prepared to pay for it to be done on a much larger scale. Unfortunately, the annual amount of spending per person on direct nature conservation in a country like Britain amounts to about the cost of a bar of chocolate. In overcrowded industrialized countries, preservation is not enough, since our environment has already been exploited by humans many times over. What is needed is a concerted rehabilitation of ecosystems long damaged by centuries of exploitation.

On the maps of many moorlands in the Scottish Highlands are printed the names of long-gone forests. What exists today could be called wet deserts, where the social and ecological damage is comparable to what is happening around the spreading edges of real deserts in hotter climes. They are the product of intense degradation, especially by intensive sheep grazing. Where businessmen shoot grouse, there is a golden opportunity to initiate a recovery of a much richer and more productive ecology than current land ownership and uses permit.

Urban areas could be far more hospitable to wild plants and animals. The migration of many creatures from the countryside to the city demonstrates how modern farming and forestry are making their previous environments uninhabitable. Some ecologically-oriented architects have designed buildings that replicate features of the land they bury. Huge scope is offered by urban wastelands, playing fields and public gardens. The expanding number of urban wildlife parks have produced far richer and more interesting habitats than those presented by the bare lawns of much urban landscaping.

Finally, greater self-reliance within urban centres could considerably reduce the pressures on land elsewhere. Many cities, especially in the Far East, produce much of their own food within their boundaries, from allotments and rooftop gardens.

HANDS OFF

Some 'ecoservices', particularly genetic diversity, can only be provided by areas of land and water kept free from all forms of human exploitation. Plans for the sustainable use of tropical rainforests, for example, will probably destroy their essential ecological character as surely as the current operations of loggers, ranchers and miners. That many National Parks cannot tolerate the pressure of recreational activities emphasizes the incompatibility of what might seem benign use and environmental conservation. Paul Ehrlich has spelled out what is necessary: 'In developed countries, disturbance of any more land should be forbidden and creation of exotic monocultures, be they golf courses, wheat fields, or tree plantations, restrained everywhere.'

Globally we should work to create a network of wilderness areas kept free from exploitation in perpetuity. They would centre on key zones such as virgin forests, especially in the tropics, swamps, watersheds, estuaries and barrier reefs, and the habitats of rare plants and animals. Antarctica is one obvious candidate. Many such areas are located where the twin pressures of population and poverty are greatest. In the Himalayas and Malaysia, local people, especially indigenous tribes, are battling to prevent further destruction from the combined actions of national government and business interests. In such cases, the rich countries must be prepared to pay if these socio-ecological pressures in poorer countries are to be defused.

9.
POWER POINTS

Standing between society and the environment are the artefacts of technology. Many people regard these as essentially neutral tools, and any failings merely a result of their misuse in the wrong hands. Greens disagree totally with that view. Different technologies not only embody different human values, but also produce different social and environmental impacts regardless of who owns them.

The choices essentially boil down to two alternatives — the 'hard' technology path or the 'soft' technology path. We can of course put a windmill next to a nuclear power plant, but in a more meaningful sense the two paths are mutually exclusive. As Hugh Nash says, a society 'cannot aspire to be both conspicuously consumptive and elegantly frugal ... the hard and the soft paths are culturally and institutionally antagonistic and furthermore, compete for the same limited resources ... a society cannot dedicate itself simultaneously to vegetarianism and cannibalism.'

Not only does conventional policy-making disregard the implications of technological choice; it reflects an almost religious faith in the power of applied science.

TECHNOFIXES ARE FLAWED

Some turn to science and technology to maintain things so that we can continue as before. Examples of this include the green revolution of hybrid high-yielding plants in agriculture to feed exploding populations; more sophisticated police hardware to combat crime; bypasses to ease traffic congestion; the diversion of rivers and the towing of icebergs to provide water; more guns and bombs to combat global insecurity; even the colonizing of the moon and outer space to solve problems here on Earth. Such 'fixes' might work for some problems for a short time. Normally, however, they compound the problem they are meant to solve. More seriously, by postponing change, technofixes will make the inevitable transition to a 'steady-state' society much harder and more unpalatable than if we made the first moves in that direction now. We cannot rely upon technofixes, because knowledge and its application are not free from constraints and costs. Some technical problems may have no solution, while others simply cost too much. All new technologies bring new risks of unforeseen side-effects which may outweigh their successes. Technologies are interdependent, and breakthroughs in one area often produce mismatches elsewhere, for example between bigger tankers and existing harbour and canal facilities.

Problems of wasteful obsolesence are often multiplied by technological innovation. Bigger technologies bring bigger problems, from the risks of breakdown, accident and error, while the greater use of hardware is often at the expense of human satisfaction and employment. Lack of foresight, time and money can all prevent technology from galloping to the rescue. In any case, as Paul Ehrlich and John Holdren comment, 'technological rabbits ... usually have large appetites and abundant noxious droppings.' Apart from the risks, technofixes are often totally irrelevant, since many of our problems are not technical at all, but are social and cultural.

The ultimate technofix is the belief in abundant cheap energy, currently centred on the prospect of nuclear fusion. Even if we could solve this technology's problems (the equivalent of recreating the conditions on the surface of the sun down here on Earth), and even if we could afford the enormous capital costs involved, the biophysical constraints would still limit its use on a scale sufficient to maintain physical expansion.

As John Holdren, Paul and Anne Ehrlich explain, energy is not the only problem: 'Food, shelter, clothing, education, and opportunity for the billions will certainly require energy, but they will also require other raw materials, social organization and co-operation, and much help from the already beleaguered processes of the biosphere.' Social organization and co-operation are themselves subject to constraints.

Energy policy is undoubtedly the most important of all technological choices. No technology more faithfully reflects social values and structures. No technology so forcefully moulds society around it. That is why it offers an ideal case study to illuminate the Green approach to the selection of technologies which are in harmony with people and their environment.

Compared to their predecessors, industrial societies use far more energy, and most of their supply comes from 'capital' rather than from 'income', from primary rather than renewable sources. We tend to think of energy purely in terms of how to supply more of it to meet ever greater demands. The real question is not the rival claims of nuclear power, fossil fuels and renewable energy. The simple truth is that present, let alone projected, levels of energy consumption are far too high.

The thirst of the industrial countries is fast depleting finite supplies of oil and gas, uranium and coal. Temporary falls in prices cannot disguise this essential fact. The transnational oil corporations have put their eggs into several baskets by investing in a range of energy options. The fate of any one energy source (and the communities dependent upon it) does not figure large in their calculations. Conservation measures could make the sources last longer, but this is only a temporary breathing space before there is a further growth in demand for energy, especially by the newly industrializing countries. Environmental degradation and pollution inevitably result from the conversion of energy from one form to another, causing pollution and also dangerously disrupting weather patterns.

All energy supply industries require physical space, none more so than solar energy conversion. Yet subsidence, spoil heaps, polluted rivers and the general devastation around coal and uranium mines result not only in immobilization, but in the wholesale destruction of the land. The dead zones around offshore oil wells, tanker accidents, blowouts, and leaks from pipelines and storage tanks threaten estuaries, seas and oceans. Increased reliance on centralized electricity generation from the conversion of primary fuels only compounds the problems. Kit Pedler once noted that the organization that runs Britain's largest power plants, the CEGB, should properly be called 'the waste heat generating company, since its prime product is entropy not electricity'.

There were protests about smoke pollution from coal fires as far back as the Middle Ages. Today lakes, soil and forests are being destroyed by the airborne acids produced by the burning of coal, oil and gas, in power stations, smelting plants and transport facilities. No civilization can survive such an assault on the productivity of the environment. Increased energy consumption will more than cancel out any abatements from chimney filters and other technological aids. Such 'fixes' do not make pollution go away, but just transfer it from one form or place to another, at the cost of yet more energy, more resource depletion and more pollution.

No technology can prevent the release of carbon dioxide into the atmosphere which inevitably accompanies the burning of fossil fuels. The result, the 'greenhouse effect', could be calamitous, causing the sea level to rise and disrupting food production as climatic patterns change. While scientists debate the details of what is happening, the severity and irreversibility of the risks involved mean that we must act now to minimize them.

THE NUCLEAR DEBATE

Acid rain and the dangers of the 'greenhouse effect' have been seized upon by a pro-nuclear lobby still reeling from the accidents at Three Mile Island and Chernobyl. To switch from reliance on fossil fuels to the nuclear option, however, is like jumping out of the frying pan into the fire. There can be few technologies that have so many sound arguments against it.

The dangers of nuclear power production include the low-level radiation routinely released as part of the nuclear fuel cycle; worse thermal pollution than that from coal-fired power plants; unsolved problems of radioactive waste disposal; the potential risk of catastrophic accidents in fuel transportation, and in power and reprocessing plants; the short lifespan and huge decommissioning problems of nuclear power stations; soaring financial costs; poor job creation per pound spent; lack of versatility in the energy supplied; the low net energy yield from the nuclear cycle, and its thermodynamic unsuitability for many end uses of energy; its irrelevance to poorer countries, especially rural and shanty town dwellers without grid electricity; the fission reactors' dependence on finite supplies of uranium whose price and political security is most uncertain; the provision of an ideal route to nuclear weapons manufacture; its vulnerability to terrorism and sabotage; and the threat to civil liberties from its strict operating requirements.

That was relatively speaking the good news. The bad news is the new fast breeder reactor cycle, by which the industry hopes to avoid the demise of nuclear fission. The resulting 'plutonium economy' would multiply all of the hazards and costs, and bring its own additional problems. Its very viability might be in doubt if reprocessing fails to recover sufficient fuel to keep the cycle going.

We should remember that these problems are created by what is a tiny industry when measured accurately in terms of delivered energy. Much attention is paid to solving these difficulties, with little progress. By comparison, alternative sources of energy have been almost totally neglected. As in any enterprise, there are examples of mismanagement and incompetence within the nuclear industry, but the intrinsic characteristics of this technology make human error uniquely perilous. Few technologies are so unforgiving.

Why did such a blighted source of electricity ever get off the ground, and why do governments struggle to keep its head above the water? The driving force has been what Pringle and Spigelman's book calls the 'nuclear barons', a clique of decision-makers united in the military-nuclear-industrial complex. Big business and centralized government favour forms of energy that are most in their own image, and none come bigger and more centralized than nuclear power. Its military connection and its role in marginalizing potentially troublesome groups such as coal miners complete its attractions. So deep are the interests vested in nuclear power that normal considerations of profit are waived.

Some sections of the public also support nuclear power. The high-tech image might appeal to those unaware or unconcerned about the realities of uranium mines or the irresponsibility of leaving unsolved problems to future generations. Hidden subsidies and unmet costs, now well documented, did help to maintain a fiction of cheapness. The siting of nuclear facilities in areas of high unemployment won it support, although this is now slipping as local people realize the danger, especially to their children.

Propagandists for the industry also deployed some deceptive arguments. Nuclear power plants were misleadingly compared with coal mines (instead of comparing one complete fuel cycle with another), while the significance of human contributions to natural background radioactivity was glossed over. Some even claimed that nuclear power was the answer to the oil crisis.

The issues are complicated. If you are reading this book warmed by an electric fire that runs off nuclear power, the fact that 85 per cent of the original potential energy has been lost in the steps between you and the uranium mine is not immediately obvious.

THE COAL PITFALL

Another Chernobyl would probably seal the fate of conventional nuclear power. However, in view of all the arguments against it

— above all our obligations to our descendants — we should initiate an immediate closure programme. The coal industry would then push for more coal-burning, which is not a satisfactory long-term alternative to the nuclear option. Apart from human health hazards, geological disturbance, water pollution, acid rain and climatic disruption, oil supplies would be further depleted by increased movement of this bulky, dirty commodity.

There is a compelling case against more centralized electricity generation by any means. This becomes clear when looking at thermodynamic efficiency, specifically the appropriate matching of different energy sources to their end uses, and more generally the amount of useful energy yielded. The American physicist Amory Lovins argues that centrally generated electricity is primarily suited to about 8 per cent of energy needs. Beyond that it is, in his much-quoted phrase, 'like using a chain saw to cut butter'.

LIMITED SCOPE FOR RENEWABLES

There are alternative sources of energy: from wind and wave power; tidal barrages; hydro-electricity; hot rocks and springs; ocean thermal gradients and solar ponds; 'energy' crops and other biomass sources of fuel; and direct harnessing of sunlight by photovoltaics, solar 'furnaces', and passive and active solar heating systems.

For nearly all its history, humanity has met its energy needs by these means. That we still do is partly disguised because much of our use of solar energies is 'free', and therefore is not reflected in statistics recording energy consumption. People who dry their clothes on the washing line rather than switch on a tumble-drier are ignored by such book-keeping, which as a result makes the transition to a solar-powered society seem more daunting. Once we think not in abstract terms but of the actual purposes energy serves, the potential of many alternatives, even of comparatively low energy quality, becomes clear.

Dreams of powering the current lifestyles of the industrialized countries from alternative energy sources are illusory, given their diffuse and variable nature. We should not disguise their technical problems, and the costs of concentration, upgrading and storage. If we take into account the fossil fuel used to manufacture the hardware for renewable technologies, little if any net energy has so far been yielded.

Schemes for large-scale hydroelectric dams, tidal barrages and monocultures of fuel crops will only perpetuate the errors inherent in a high-energy society, and should therefore be avoided. Business and governments have shown most interest in enormous wind turbine and wave machines, technologies that most closely match the prevailing vision of industrialism. But that is not the promise of solar power. As Andrew Mackillop and Peter Bunyard comment, 'it is not the quantity of energy available that matters but the use we make of it ... To ask whether the sun, the wind and the waves can replace all the energy currently supplied by fossil fuels is to pose the wrong question. We must ask instead how these resources can be most effectively used to facilitate the changeover from an industrial to a post-industrial society.' Renewability does not in itself make an energy technology more socially and ecologically appropriate than one based upon finite sources.

THE WRONG PATH: MORE ENERGY FROM MORE CENTRALIZED SOURCES

Increased energy consumption is inseparably linked to centralized production. One fuels the other. Together they trigger many changes. In the USA ecologist Kenneth Watt has charted a series of 'causal pathways' flowing from centralized production. They include the encouragement of further energy use by large users, unstable trading relationships, more health hazards and greater health care costs, more unemployment, more economic inequality and more inflation. The economies of scale create diseconomies all around them. Amory Lovins has estimated that for small consumers only 29 per cent of their electricity costs are for actual electricity; the rest is for transmission, distribution equipment, and maintenance.

A high-energy society is both ecologically impossible to sustain, and socially undesirable. There is no relation between rising *per capita* energy consumption and more human happiness. Such consumption requires very complicated and centralized technologies, and therefore complex management structures. These come at a price: less democracy, less local autonomy, less freedom of information and civil liberty, and less social equity. This is self-evidently true of nuclear power because of the security measures required, but it could be even more so if heavy demands were placed on renewable energy sources, with the complicated management this would require.

Professor Wilcox has described the 'cruel paradox' whereby high-energy technologies create a social culture that undermines the human qualities on which their smooth running depends. Cheap and plentiful power tempts society to gross excess.

In a centralized, high-energy society, benefits and costs are separated to an unprecedented extent. The consequences of

Chernobyl were less critical to users of its electricity than to innocent people living nearby, thousands of miles away, or even in future generations. This problem is not confined to the nuclear industry. Sami reindeer herders were suffering long before Chernobyl because of the drowning of their valleys to supply Norwegian cities with hydroelectric power. In America, the lands and well-being of the Hopi and Navajo Indians are being destroyed by opencast coal mining and power complexes to keep the lights of Las Vegas burning. The soft energy path is the only one that will stop one group from making others foot the real costs of its energy bill.

FOLLOWING THE SOFT ENERGY PATH

Professor Miles has summed up society's choice: 'Our options are either to plunge ahead from our petroleum addiction to a plutonium addiction, or to recognize our energy binge for what it has been, turn over a new leaf, and seek to develop a new moderate-energy civilization, based ultimately upon living within the annual budget of energy that comes from the sun.'

The wind will continue to blow, water will flow and the sun will shine regardless of human actions. We can satisfy our needs today from these sources without robbing future generations of their energy supply. Solar technologies have other great advantages. They do not disrupt the planet's heat balance. The burning of fossil fuels, and nuclear fission and fusion, add heat to the environment. Every increase brings us closer to the critical point where damaging changes in climate and in global flora and fauna are triggered. This ultimate pollutant would limit the use of nuclear fusion even if all its other drawbacks could be overcome. In marked contrast, solar energy sources are a use of, not an addition to, the earth's natural heat balance and therefore create no significant disturbance.

The sunshine falls virtually everywhere, so solar energies are appropriate for self-reliant, decentralized and democratic societies. Social vulnerability to disruption would be correspondingly reduced. The relative simplicity of these tried and tested technologies makes them amenable to individual and public control. Communities should directly benefit from *and* face the true costs of their mix of energy technologies, a positive incentive to wise decision-making.

SAVE ... SAVE ... SAVE ...

Energy conservation in its fullest sense is crucial. This means more than insulation, efficient equipment and processes, and the use of technologies such as heat pumps and cogeneration power systems. It also means the general elimination of waste and unnecessary production in the economy. Society must cut its coat according to its limited energy cloth.

Professor Polesynski of Oslo University has estimated potential savings of as much as 80-90 per cent, especially by what he calls 'trimming off the fat' of military expenditure, space exploration, the car industry, food processing and packaging, marketing, pharmaceuticals, cosmetic and fashion products and areas of international trade where virtually identical products are exchanged over great distances.

The switch to the soft energy path is the simplest, cheapest, safest and quickest way out of the so-called choice between coal and nuclear power. The first step would be the closure of all nuclear plants. The timescale in which this could be done is a minor technicality. No further large coal-fired power stations would be constructed. Instead priority would be given to many small-scale combined heat and power plants in local communities, and to industrial cogeneration schemes, including heat pumps, in larger enterprises and public buildings. Scandinavian countries have already started along that road.

A particular target would be electrical resistance space heating. Discounts would cease for large users, and all energy advertising apart from conservation would immediately stop. Research and development would be redirected to conservation and technologies for the small-scale harnessing and storage of solar energy flows. Fiscal policy and building regulations would be progressively revised to discriminate in favour of a low-energy, solar-powered society. Surplus capacity in industries such as shipbuilding would be used for the production of soft energy hardware.

In line with basic Green principles, energy resources should belong to the public, as should pipelines and electrical transmission systems. The warring interests of gas, coal, oil and electricity would be united under regional energy authorities. Locally, district agencies would be responsible for energy audits, the stimulation of conservation measures, and the longer-term planning of the change to more benign and ambient energy sources. The pioneering work of some American communities provides an exemplary model.

Public loans would be made available to enable consumers to offset the comparatively high initial costs of conservation measures and the installation of solar technologies. The agencies themselves could be the central purchasing vehicle. The transition cannot be left to the free market which is biased towards short-term calculations, discounting sustainability, lifetime costs and ultimate efficiency.

Green policies, especially resource depletion quotas or resource taxes, will push up energy prices. Many people fear that higher fuel bills would worsen the effects of hypothermia on elderly citizens unable to afford to stay warm, but their plight should not be the excuse to make energy cheap for profligate use. Instead, those in need should be subsidized to overcome such problems. When it is understood that cheap energy has displaced people in one field of production after another, the positive benefits of Green policy become clearer. It is recognized that a programme of energy conservation would create more jobs, but the ripple effects would spread much further once energy is realistically costed.

For their own sakes, industralized countries must halt their growth in energy consumption, and then reduce it. This is also a vital procondition if the problems of global poverty are to be addressed. Planet Earth cannot tolerate everyone using more energy.

Green energy policy — CARE (conservation and renewable energy) — not only recognizes these limits, but opens the door to exciting new prospects for an energy base appropriate to real human fulfilment throughout the world.

10.
ECO-NOMICS

To medieval people the construction of a cathedral like Notre Dame in Paris was a perfectly rational thing to do. Nowadays it would be dismissed as 'uneconomic', and this dreaded and solemn word would close the argument. Banks and government treasuries hold the whip-hand in decision-making in every sphere of life, and the ideology of economics is paramount.

This framework, which dominates mainstream economic theory, mirrors general intellectual changes, and notably the acceptance of a purely 'objective' approach to reality. Beneath this scientific exterior are a series of assumptions about human nature and the capacities of the environment. Henryk Skolimowski has documented some of these premises: human psychology as aggressive and selfish; culture as just another useful commodity; society as nothing more than a conglomerate of individuals; progress as the ever-expanding consumption of material goods; efficiency as the making of more monetary profit; technology as the midwife of prosperity and happiness; and nature as an endless treasure chest, there for the taking.

Economic models from the Marxist to the monetarist share many of these premises. Above all they share the same goal — greater material consumption. Economic policies derived from such models, whether in the USSR or the USA, are undermining the viability of society. To see why, we need to look more closely at the fallacies behind the concept of growth: ever increasing physical throughput of energy, materials and information in the economy, and the creation of ever more goods and services.

LIMITS TO ECONOMIC EXPANSION

Mainstream economic thinking has constructed an unecological model of reality, based on the notion of an endless cycle of supply and demand. These two might be brought together by state planning or by the market economy, but the assumption is the same. Consequently production and consumption are not rooted in the realities of the biophysical world.

Assessed in the light of the ecological limits to growth, the fashionable notion of 'sustainable growth' in material wealth is a contradiction. Human satisfaction can certainly increase with no adverse ecological consequence. But the evidence of drug addiction and crimes of violence, of mental stress and marital breakdown suggests that individual and communal well-being are in fact being threatened by the values and behaviour patterns that accompany economic 'growthmania'. Boosting consumer demand depends on the expansion of credit and debt, creating new economic instabilities.

In materially affluent societies consumption becomes increasingly oriented toward what have been called 'positional goods', a constant chase to keep up with our fellow citizens. The process is self-defeating, since competition for status, style and amenities becomes more elusive as more people aspire to them. We cannot all be relatively better off.

Some supporters of economic expansion argue that growth is necessary to pay for social and environmental advance. The lesson of the limits-to-growth model is that the harmful side-effects expand at a faster rate than any tax revenues accrue for financing solutions. Disastrously, some results of economic growth, from habitat destruction to exhausted resources, cannot be put right by any amount of spending.

MYTHS OF THE MARKET

What rival purchasers are prepared to spend on a particular item may indicate how much they value it. At that level, the market mechanism is a quick and efficient tool for expressing individual preferences. Bureaucratic devices such as rationing, by contrast, tend to be cumbersome, expensive, and prone to corruption.

As a basis for social decision-making, however, the virtues of buying and selling are offset by many vices. Bidding can only take place between bidders, and therefore the market only reflects the preferences of those alive today. Those with enough money can command that foodstuffs are grown to feed their pets rather than starving human beings. The needs of those yet to be born cannot be expressed in such a setting. It cannot cope with absolute scarcities, nor can it deal with commodities upon which it is impossible to put a price, such as clean air.

Truly free markets have never existed for any length of time, nor ever will. The inbuilt tendency for larger economic units to drive out smaller ones creates conditions in which the rules of the market are drawn up to suit the major enterprises that dominate it.

Political decisions are necessary to set the limits in which market mechanisms can operate. It is not a question of state planning *or* a free market, but of creating an ecological framework to guide the overall economy. Within this framework what matters is what is most appropriate — public or private provision, individual or collective enterprise. Water supply, for example, is best kept in public hands, because its provision is essential to life; the supply of shirts, on the other hand, is better left to private initiative and creativity.

LONG—TERM SOLUTIONS

Green economic institutions would be based on the rules of true housekeeping: conserving the Earth. Garrett Hardin puts the issue squarely: 'In a world of limits we can become wealthy only if we subject ourselves to the discipline of demand control ... Confronted with a painful discrepancy between supply and demand, the prisoners of a squanderarchy invariably speak of a shortage of supply. Why do they never speak of a longage of demand? ... To speak of "shortage" is to predispose the mind to look only for ways to increase supply. By speaking of "longage" we force our minds to consider the possibility of decreasing demand'.

The thread that links all aspects of a Green economic policy is the shift of revenue-raising away from activities such as recycling and repair work, towards those which discourage excessive use (and waste) of energy and raw materials. These include community ground rent, primarily designed to discourage speculation over land; progressive income tax; a progressive turnover tax on companies to encourage smaller businesses; and selective purchase taxes on luxury goods.

A crucial long-term reform would be to break the monopoly power of private banks over the creation of money, and their parasitic role in making fictitious profits (profits not backed up by real physical resources) out of other people's debts. In their place would be a network of locally accountable community banks.

Such policies recall Jeremy Rifkin's words: 'The most important truth about ourselves, our artefacts and our civilization is that it is all borrowed ... We are forever borrowing from the environment to create and maintain the totality of our way of life. Everything we transform eventually ends up back in nature after we have expropriated whatever temporary value we can from it.' Unlike the models of Adam Smith and his followers, such insights point us to the task of maintaining the *real* wealth of nations.

11.
CONSUMERISM

'Consumer sovereignty' is one of the hallowed shrines of mainstream economic theory. 'Shopping around' will, we are told, avoid the bad aspects of the market economy. Human needs are equated with the purchase of commodities, and all we have to do is rationally to select those which best match our needs. Happiness is ours for the buying.

The reality is different. With the volume and rapidly changing range of products on the market, many with specifications comprehensible only to the expert, an individual's judgment is inadequate. Even experts do not know the potential consequences of many of the complex chemical substances in some of today's manufactured goods. Even with all the relevant information, consumer choice can be a time-consuming process, and when the right product is identified, the price may be beyond the consumer's means. We need a collective rather than a private approach, in which society sets appropriate parameters for the quantity and quality of goods and services available.

SPEND ... SPEND ... SPEND

Linking mass production and mass consumption is the advertising industry. This bombards us daily with messages about every area of life. The public images of leading politicians are as carefully managed as those of toilet cleansers, and are often as accurate.

Relatively minor among the costs of advertising are the direct financial ones, many of them passed straight on to the public. More serious is the imbalance in access to the 'means of persuasion'. The management of public opinion and consumer spending is monopolized by and for those with the most money: just compare the resources devoted to the sale of cigarettes with those deployed to discourage smoking. It becomes more dangerous when the communication is not about actual facts and figures, but the subtle weaving of seductive images around a product or an institution.

The dynamics of advertising add to the social and ecological disruptions from mass industrialism, and not just because they exploit our hopes and fears by harnessing them to the purchase of a particular commodity. Advertising delivers well-tutored consumers to the shop counter. Modern ideas about marketing developed hand in hand with the growth of mass-production. Both depend on discouraging self-reliance on one's own resources and judgment. Marketing people actually study human psychology, to identify feelings that can be converted to needs, which can in turn be commercialized. Drug companies might compete to sell you a headache cure, but are united in working to ensure you do not find a non-drug solution.

Advertising dangles new (or repackaged) products before the consumers' eyes, promising satisfaction. Then the story starts again as newer goods and services come on line. Who we are and what we own become blurred in a world of style, fashion and image. And as Fred Hirsch shows, consumer advertising sells best when appealing to individuals to look after themselves and their immediate family. That is, it maximizes self-concern at the expense of social cohesion.

While causing individual insecurity, mass advertising also promotes external insecurity, in the ecology. Notions such as durability, reduced or shared consumption, or substituting non-material pleasures for the use of objects, conflict with the requirements of mass marketing. Advertising is tied to an expanding economy, the one thing that we, living on a finite planet, must avoid.

The message of advertising is always more consumption. It disfigures landscapes and townscapes. It encourages waste, from unnecessary model changes to gimmicks which supposedly differentiate identical products. Its bottom line can only be environmental destruction. This in turn can become a marketing opportunity, as the consequent scarcity of open space, wildlife or clean streams is turned into a chance to market what still survives, or to sell technological 'substitutes'.

CONSUMER RIGHTS?

Contemporary consumer movements reflect the values of the individual as maximizing consumer, rather than as co-operating citizen. Magazines and television reports discuss which of several items is the 'best buy'. No mention is made of the resources used up in their manufacture, the boredom and health hazards of their production lines, reusability or recyclability, nor pollution. They seldom ask whether the items are necessary, or whose interests and priorities they serve. Electric salad shakers are, in the consumer test lab, as worthy a use of natural resources and human creativity as anything else. The constant priority is more consumer choice from an ever-increasing number of products to sell.

Consumer organizations have made constructive suggestions for improving the legislation about the description and sale of goods. What they seem unable to comprehend is how little this has to do with real self-determination and self-reliance, concepts alien to the whole consumerist ethic.

LESS PRESSURE-SELLING

Many high quality products seem to sell themselves, often by word-of-mouth recommendation. Restricting mass marketing will benefit reputable manufacturers, consumers and the environment alike. There need to be three types of control. The first is quantitative, reducing the volume of marketing by ending large-scale advertising as a legitimate expense, and by progressively taxing all expenditure on sales promotion above a minimum level. This recognizes that some advertising is concerned with information, and is therefore not necessarily undesirable.

The second problem is the techniques of persuasion, and the imagery and language of advertisements. The present regulation system lacks both independence and teeth. We need to find a more comprehensive set of standards and means of enforcement. Following the example of cigarette advertisements, one idea would be to require full information in publicity and packaging — for example pollution warnings on phosphate washing powders.

How, though, can we lay down precise standards for meanings in messages? Some products pose special threats to people or the environment. Here all forms of advertising, including sponsorship, would be immediately prohibited. This would cover cars, airlines, energy supply, drugs, and meat products. For the first three, the reason is the resource depletion, environmental pollution and safety hazards from their manufacture and use. Exemptions could be allowed to announce cleaner, safer or more frugal specifications. The advertising of energy-saving techniques, for example, would be encouraged.

The consequences of promoting drug consumption among the general public have already been mentioned. The problem of the army of pharmaceutical sales reps, with free samples and promotional items aimed at medical practitioners, is more complicated. A special unit of an office of technology assessment to deal with new medicines might be the proper channel to communicate appropriate innovations to the medical world at large.

High levels of meat consumption waste food resources, and cause environmental damage, cruelties and health hazards. On the same TV channels, within a few minutes of each other, we see news of famine and advertisements trying to persuade us to eat more meat products. Such advertisements should be banned.

We have not yet mentioned advertising aimed at children. The problem is not so much the products themselves as the nature of the audience. Programmes are used as vehicles to push some new toy, while many advertisements promoting sugar seem designed to create jobs for dentists. Packaging and free gifts with food items such as breakfast cereals pervert nutritional sense, and make the responsible parent's job harder. Similar controls need to be applied in those areas.

12.
MAKING A LIVING

Rising human numbers and rising levels of consumption have made it impossible for all but a handful of people in favourable places to be self-sufficient. We now depend on a range of trading relationships. Under industrialism, the most important of these is how we sell our mental and physical labour to others, and nowadays many people define themselves by the job they do. This mechanism for making a living, however, is breaking down under the pressure of social, economic and technological change.

The heart of the problem is the way in which society chains livelihood to the tenure of a full-time paid job. Productive work is similarly defined — and confined. Countless people in jobs are frustrated because there are so many more enjoyable and truly productive things they could be doing with their time, yet those without jobs are often desperate for such employment, to escape the misery of being without the income and social status of paid work.

At the same time, willing and able hands remain idle or harmfully employed, while a great many urgent and useful tasks, not least in the fields of resource conservation and environmental protection, are not getting done. Often, desirable and continuing projects cannot provide full-time jobs since they consist of a mass of 'bits and pieces'. At best they receive superficial attention from community schemes, often designed to make the unemployment registers seem shorter. Some are ignored totally, despite their importance to long-term sustainability.

THE FALLACIES OF FULL EMPLOYMENT

Technological change is paving the way for a radical restructuring of how people can provide for themselves. Government policies might boost or lower the level of unemployment at any one time, but this does not alter the underlying reality. Our technological systems are now so productive that they can provide sufficient goods and services for society using a comparatively small and decreasing percentage of its workforce.

In these circumstances slogans about 'No Return to the 30s' and 'Jobs For All' are irrelevant if not downright reactionary. The very concept of permanent full-time employment denigrates the contribution of those who, for various reasons, are outside the economy of formal paid work. It reflects a redundant notion of lifestyles based on a cycle of school-employment-retirement. It does not understand that attempts to launch job-creating economic booms must eventually run up against ecological and human limits to growth. All this does is to create quick profits which go to finance more automation and job destruction. We simply cannot produce our way out of unemployment.

Boom or bust economic policies are not the only conventional response to the issues of employment and livelihood. Some have tried feather-bedding lame duck enterprises, others manipulate statistics to make unemployment levels seem artificially smaller. Particularly harmful are the increasing number of mechanisms to keep the old and the young out of the labour market. Arbitrary retirement dates keep people in jobs when they want to leave and force people out when they could happily and productively stay. Raising the school-leaving age confines many youngsters to an environment they would choose to leave if only there were better opportunities outside.

Many people suggest cuts in the working week or the working year, as a way of creating more jobs. However, further automation and overtime working can quickly soak up hours released by these measures. Earlier voluntary retirement faces the same obstacles, and brings the additional problems of higher pension costs and lost tax revenue.

To entice employers to retain old jobs or create new ones, proponents of permanent full-time employment disregard such considerations as workers' rights and environmental standards. Trade unions and their political representatives offer support to arms manufacturers, retailers of radiation, and purveyors of pollution. Capital is more mobile than labour, and its owners can relocate their activities despite local opposition. Ordinary workers often have no alternative but to defend wasteful and harmful production processes to save their livelihoods.

Labour organizations are sometimes worse than employers in their opposition to innovations such as job-sharing. Yet these can offer many people, especially women, more satisfactory ways of reconciling the commitments and ambitions in their lives.

BAD WORK IF YOU CAN GET IT

The deskilling of more and more tasks, combined with health and safety hazards, make much employment anything but liberating and fulfilling. This is an inevitable consequence of our reliance on production-maximizing technologies which trivialize human labour.

Its roots go deeper than the form of ownership — it has happened in capitalist and communist countries alike. The poor quality and decreasing quantity of work stem from the large-scale use of energy and material resources in modern society. More enlightened firms have attempted 'job enrichment' schemes for their workforces, yet boring occupations do not become more satisfying just by rotating them. While it might be more fulfilling to be involved in the construction of a product from start to finish, real progress depends upon its social and environmental value. Even full-time jobs that are demonstrably useful and organized along democratic lines may still seriously restrict a person's way of life. Much more flexible arrangements are necessary if we are to reconcile personal obligations with greater individual freedom.

GAPING HOLES IN AN EXPENSIVE NET

Modern social security was undoubtedly a great step forward after the evils of the poor house, but it was founded on false assumptions about economic growth and employment. Government priming of the economy would, it was believed, make unemployment something that was marginal and temporary, and the benefits system was designed accordingly. The more the queues of the long-term unemployed have lengthened, the more the system's shortcomings have become evident. Not even so-called full employment solved the problems of insecurity and poverty, but recent changes in work patterns have exposed gaping holes in the social security net.

The net itself requires an enormous and expensive bureaucracy to administer the mass of rules which dictate who gets what and when. Claimants are treated not as citizens receiving what is theirs by right, but as supplicants for state handouts. There are doubtless some 'scroungers' who abuse the system. Far more people, however, are simply not getting money to which they are entitled because of the hurdles built into the system. Charity-style handouts for the needy contrast with the virtual free-for-all at the other end of the social spectrum, where the rich can employ expense accounts and tax evasion to make themselves richer. The fiddlers on the roof of society cost us far more than any petty fraud below stairs.

DEVALUED

The linking of status and income with formal employment, and the power that both bring, devalue all the unpaid and voluntary work performed in the home and the community. As Michael Bassey has noted about Britain, it is not just those in paid jobs but some '34 million workers [who] create the quality of life by which 56 million people live, the non-workers being aged people and children'. Those who work in the home are one group who suffer from conventional valuations of who does what. As Bassey says, 'caring for one's own children in the home is work no more or no less than caring for other people's children in a nursery'. The so-called 'invisible' economy might allow people to evade financial obligations to society, but in many other ways it has kept individuals, communities and in some cases entire countries from economic collapse.

LIMITLESS LEISURE

One of the biggest political deceptions of all is the notion of a dawning leisure society, when what is in fact envisaged is compulsory idleness. Leisure has become one of the fastest growth industries, turning what were the free enjoyments of yesterday into commodities for sale tomorrow — to those who can afford them.

Amusement centres and theme parks proliferate, along with family days out at suburban shopping complexes. Here we meet the newest recruits to the ranks of the 'disabling professions', the leisure managers. Where once people would entertain themselves, regimentation is fast becoming the norm. Instead of creative, free activities, the leisure society would further spread what Murray Bookchin called the 'banalization and impoverishment of experience'.

The world of organized leisure is as status-ridden as that of work, offering little repose from the stresses of organized labour. The greatest social danger from any leisure society is its corrosion of the human spirit. People are robbed of involvement in the social production of useful goods and services. This is, in Fritz Schumacher's words, to be 'in service to, and in co-operation with, others, so as to liberate ourselves from our inborn egocentricity'. People need to feel useful.

Leisure also poses new threats to the environment. From the concrete jungles of the Mediterranean to the paraphernalia of ski resorts, industrialized leisure has consumed ever more space, energy and materials, has degraded soil and vegetation, and caused air, water, noise and aesthetic pollution. Yet the economy will never be able to grow sufficiently to give everyone access to the trappings of beach buggies and such consumerist hardware. Thus for many the promised leisure society will deliver little more than passive spectating, and the resulting envy will give another twist to the spiral of anti-social feelings.

A BASIC INCOME SCHEME

The alternative is to clear aside the morass of handouts and clawbacks. The Green approach is to abolish all existing welfare benefits, tax allowances, and grants. Every citizen would receive instead a basic income sufficient for their essential needs. It would be protected by indexation, to compensate for productivity changes and inflation. It would be given to everyone, in or out of paid employment and regardless of household structure. There would simply be a unified payment, one rate for adults and one for the first two children. The more that such a system is complicated by additional benefits and associated regulations, the more its efficiency and fairness is compromised.

The rationalization of the way in which society supports its citizens would be matched by changes in how citizens contribute financially to society. Employers' and employees' national insurance contributions would be abolished, and tax would be levied on a progressive basis on all sources and types of income, from paid work to capital transfer.

Such a basic income scheme would benefit individual, society and environment alike. It would significantly reduce the negative impact that humans are making on the rest of nature. As Warren Johnson comments, 'guaranteed income ... offers a positive incentive for reduced production, for slowing the speed of our economic train'. Fuel-efficient and long-lasting cars, for example, reduce jobs at car plants and garages. A shift to mass transit systems would cut them further.

The dependence of so many full-time jobs on an increasing output of goods and services has caused an addiction to economic growth, regardless of whether we need the produce or can tolerate its destructive effect on society and environment. The basic income scheme would ease that pressure, since people would be able to live in an economy that was no longer demanding more and more land, energy and materials. Resource depletion, pollution and environmental degradation would all be reduced. The scheme would also promote projects that help to heal past damage: with temporary and part-time jobs more attractive, environmental protection and restoration would provide plenty of opportunities.

SPRINGING TRAPS

Costs to both society and the individual would be reduced with the basic income scheme. Administrative overheads would be cut drastically, because the scheme is an unconditional payment to everyone. There would be less need for costly and powerful bureaucracies and government departments. Controls over minimum wages and maximum numbers of working years could be abolished.

The costs of the present system to the individual are psychological as well as financial. The cruel anomalies of the 'poverty trap' would disappear. The present system penalizes those who take on a low-waged job by deducting money in the form of lost benefits. The basic income scheme is paid regardless of earnings, so individuals would always gain from any paid work they could find. The 'spendthrift trap' would also go, since savings would no longer be penalized by loss of eligibility for grants and allowances. The 'idleness trap' would end, since the basic income would continue to be paid to people who want to do voluntary work, study, or launch a small business. The 'cohabitation trap' and other forms of prying into people's private lives would cease, because the scheme makes no distinctions about the way in which individuals organize their personal relationships. The 'discrimination trap' by which women, especially married women, are sometimes treated by the system as appendages to men, would end, since the scheme would guarantee economic independence for women.

In general, the stigma attached to unemployment and welfare handouts would break down, since everyone would start from the same equal footing. 'Signing on' would be ended. Those whose work is caring for children, caring for the sick and elderly, or looking after the home, would be fully recognized and rewarded. One married partner might go out to a paid job while the other worked in the home, yet both would be 'breadwinners'.

MORE WORK, BETTER WORK

The basic income scheme rationalizes a chaotic system into one that is fair and efficient, and it guarantees sufficient resources for basic security. Low-income families would gain the most. Though there are as many definitions of a 'good' standard of living as there are people, most would still want extra money from paid work, and society would still need their labour. What would change is the flexibility of matching people to work, and also the variety, quantity and quality of jobs.

The Green approach would make possible more diversity in

employer/employee arrangements, including part-timing and job-sharing, and would increase self-employment. In many ways it is a job liberation scheme. The security of guaranteed income would reduce the demand for full-time employment and stimulate a greater sharing-out of paid work. Jobs that currently offer low pay would become more attractive, since the welfare poverty trap would no longer exist. Many workers' co-operatives would be able to survive instead of collapsing. Cyclical unemployment from the ups and downs of business activity would diminish, since the scale and regularity of basic income payments would help smooth out consumer demand.

Similarly beneficial effects would result from the strictly progressive nature of Green taxation policies. These would give an incentive for those with too much work to pass part of their employment to someone else. The abolition of national insurance would end what is in effect a tax on jobs. If necessary, such measures could be augmented by tax exemptions for each additional worker an employer takes on. The economic institutions of a conserver society would encourage enterprises to substitute human labour for energy and machines, in order to save resources and cut pollution. Studies such as Edward Barbier's *Earthworks* suggest many new jobs could be created in this way.

Employers would be forced to improve pay and conditions for hazardous or monotonous jobs, because potential workers would be less pressured into taking them. In the longer term, we envisage people putting together a 'portfolio' of different activities, not just to bring in money but to provide personal development. We would anticipate that the most common social situation would become the one which, according to surveys in France, the majority of the public would most like: households where both partners work part-time and share domestic responsibilities. The basic income scheme thus offers both job liberation and social liberation.

People would be able to allocate themselves more free time in a Green economy. As André Gorz points out, 'freed time is nothing but empty time unless accompanied by other changes'. He stresses the role of co-operatively owned facilities and tools, such as workshops where paid instructors help members of the public to make or repair things for themselves. The provision of these by local authorities would enable people to rediscover a greater self-reliance in their lives.

Two categories involve some form of supplement to the basic income scheme. There are those who, for reasons of disability, sickness or old age, are not able to find paid work. And there is the problem of finding a fair way for society to help people to buy or rent accommodation. Among supporters of the basic income scheme, the most popular idea is a regionally adjusted payment of a 'housing addition' to replace mortgage relief and rent rebates.

Further detailed study is needed on the scheme — the principle of regional weightings, for example, perpetuates regional distortions. However they are formulated, such supplements should be kept separate from the basic payment. The economic efficiency, bureaucratic simplicity and social equity of the basic income scheme depend upon it not being burdened with complications. To be politically attractive, the level of basic income must save people from poverty. Beyond that, it is a matter of careful calculation of what society can afford.

It is *not* a scheme to subsidize those who shirk their social responsibilities by 'dropping out' at other people's expense. The problem of people choosing not to work, to the detriment of socially necessary production and of government revenue, is a real one. Though changes in the level of basic income could provide a means to manipulate the numbers of would-be paid workers, there are limits to this if we are not to infringe on its basic role of ensuring social stability and personal security.

Like any other policy, the basic income scheme must be financed. This would involve a reallocation of existing expenditures, such as welfare benefits and tax allowances. However, the cost of improving the current inadequate levels of social security payments plus the loss of revenue from the abolition of national insurance will require extra money. To a large extent, this will come from savings inherent in the scheme — the reduced cost of administration, and the abolition of support for third and subsequent children.

Other savings would result from the increased number of jobs, many of them part-time, bringing increased tax revenue. Many in the informal economy who do not now disclose their income (it is in effect taxed at 100 per cent through loss of benefits) would find that in the new system the risks of tax evasion outweigh gains, and this would bring in further revenue. Special purchase taxes on luxury goods such as large cars, freezers, and video equipment would all raise revenue, as would the cancellation of perks which senior executives in public and private companies award themselves at public expense. Progressive income tax would be based not on bands but on a rising scale, which would plateau at the point where society decides that income differentials have become incompatible with communal harmony.

You may wonder why a scheme so full of potential benefits has not been introduced before. The reasons are twofold. First, there are the disadvantages of current forms of part-time work, which is treated as second-class labour. Some of these might be redressed by legislation, but many result from the prejudices of those in full-time work. Second, there are the vested interests of organizations such as employers and trade unions. The former might find their profits squeezed once they had to rectify poor pay and conditions to attract people who were guaranteed a basic income, while the latter draw their income largely from existing patterns of employment. Moreover, the 'unemployment industry' itself thrives upon current circumstances. A basic income scheme could not be introduced without breaking the stranglehold of such bodies.

13.
REGIONAL DECLINE

History is littered with cities and regions that rose to power and then fell into decline, often because they abused the environment upon which they depended. The pace of economic expansion and technological change has brought an unprecedented scale and intensity to the cycle. Industrialism has created the first global economy. Multinational businesses and governments have created a new dimension to the location of labour, in which whole regions and communities have become dispensable cogs in a universal economic machine. The fate of a community, region or even state can be decided by decisions taken thousands of miles away.

The very dynamism of the industrial growth society encourages expansion first in one area and then, as cheap resources are used up or new technology renders them unnecessary, it moves on to new supplies and markets. It can shed regions as readily as it can shed workers, both victims of a restless, never-ending search for economies of scale.

Once booming areas go into decline. Some places have been up and back down again several times this century. Such an unstable process leaves behind it a trail of environmental destruction and social disruption. The old industrial heartlands of Europe and North America show similar scars, while the new boom areas — America's sunshine belt and the golden triangle of the Common Market — bear the signs of explosive growth, consuming land, resources and stable long-established communities.

The discrepancies between areas of affluence and poverty in the world economy are paralleled by similar gulfs within countries. Declining regions are frequently dependent on single industries and even single companies, just as much poorer countries are dependent upon single crops.

Attempts to relieve regional distress may be well-meaning, yet they often mistakenly look backwards to the age of mass industrialization for a solution. An example of the dangers of putting economic eggs into an already worn basket is the doomed steel smelter at Invergordon in northern Scotland, where much public money, in the form of grants and subsidies, has gone straight to the very transnational corporations whose strength is sapping regional resilience. In the North East of England, two of the region's biggest job-cutting companies (ICI and BSC) took 25 per cent of all regional development spending in the mid-1980s.

Simply transferring the funds to smaller firms does not in itself help. In a climate of regional decline, most are doomed to failure. Some new jobs are being created in these areas, but their numbers become insignificant as soon as a major employer sheds yet more workers. Regional organizations fight each other, effectively to bribe foreign companies to open plants in their localities. As a result the public is paying to import foreign industry which, once in operation, exports its profits. Comparatively few jobs are created per pound spent. With automation, big industries are rarely big employers, yet public grants often go to finance further automation. Meanwhile industrial plants and offices that are outposts of organizations based far away are nearly always the first to be cut in any reorganization.

Can deregulation and free enterprise cure these ills? Would planning controls which try to limit environmental damage stifle initiative? It is the market mechanisms that create the problems in the first place, and the main initiative which large companies display is often the tapping of the public purse. The 'freedom of enterprise' that brings firms to a region is the same freedom that allows them to take public money, and then restructure or re-locate elsewhere.

Many pin their hopes on small businesses. Among their merits is that their smallness means that comparatively few people are affected if they fail. Still, many of the new self-employed are the ex-employed, not the ex-unemployed. Co-operative ventures often cannot compete in a system loaded in favour of industrial conglomerates. A great deal of public money has gone into new roads and airports, and green belt controls have been relaxed for 'executive' homes, to entice employers into declining areas. This often merely facilitates greater movement of goods and services into an area at the expense of local production and employment.

Conventional measures seem to have failed completely in halting the haemorrhage of regional vitality in areas that become peripheral to industry's new heartlands. Environmentalists sometimes find themselves opposing schemes that promise job creation in places desperate for work. Closer examination shows that public money has in fact been paying for the decimation of both jobs and the environment.

Reversing regional decay must involve facing up to the multinational corporations. No country or region can achieve stability as long as these economic 'nations' are able to shift their operations around to suit their interests at the expense of local people and the local environment. Directing grants and subsidies away from them and towards local initiatives would help to meet local needs. Businesses receiving assistance would have to sign declarations undertaking good practice in such matters as equal opportunities and environmental protection.

A GREEN REVIVAL

Green policies including a turnover tax on the size of an enterprise would give smaller organizations a chance to flourish. Rather than trying to rekindle the industrial revolution, public money should be allocated to preparing the way for the 'solar transition'. Encouragement would be given to: combined heat and power schemes; manufacturers of equipment for renewable energy and conservation; craft industries; appropriate reafforestation and associated industries; conversion to organic farming; and land reclamation.

An overall strategy of 'import substitution' would create regional economies that are both self-reliant and sustainable. Schemes for local currencies such as the Guernsey experiment and the LET System in British Columbia, Canada, suggest that this might be a worthwhile innovation. As Jane Jacobs points out in her study of separatism, the fluctuations of national currencies tend to benefit some regions while harming others. Local currencies would help to insulate a region's fortunes against speculation on the world's financial exchanges.

As part of regional renewal, greater understanding of a region's capacities and limits would be necessary. In the 1970s would discourage projects in areas that are already over-developed or where other considerations, such as the conservation of prime agricultural land, are paramount. Major projects like the Channel Tunnel between England and France will intensify, not reduce, regional imbalance.

One obvious argument against the Green policies of regional revival is that other regions and countries, hoping to attract investment from big business, will persist in the old self-destructive practices, and could flourish at the expense of regions striving for autonomy. This is a problem that faces any attempt to change the *status quo.* The successes within the present system, such as the Mondragon co-operative network in northern Spain, suggest that progress is not impossible. In some ways, an ecological society might be in a stronger position because it would simply not need some of the products of the multinationals. It need not be the end of the world because, say, Coca-Cola take their business elsewhere.

It is difficult to envisage the viability of 'ecology in one country (or region)'. Hope for the future rests upon action for radical change that crosses boundaries. The international growth of the movements for peace, decentralism and environmental protection suggests there can be a real basis for optimism.

14.
SHARING AND
CARING

Personal fulfilment and meaning in life depend on the fulfilment of a variety of material and non-material needs. They range from food and clothing to love and affection. Satisfying them depends on three relationships. There are interpersonal relations, between one person and another. There is the inter-play between the individual and society as a whole. Both of these hinge upon getting right the third relationship, that between people and planet. There can be no 'good life', whatever its ingredients, if we disrupt those ecological cycles and flows on which the well-being of society depends. The only satisfactory approach to social organization is a holistic one which integrates all three relationships.

RIGHTS TO MORE RIGHTS

This century has witnessed an ever-lengthening shopping list of human rights. The United Nations has been foremost in calling for more entitlements for the individual. Most of these rights, however, are to be met by more goods and services. These in turn can only be produced by more demands on an already depleted and polluted Earth. Human entitlements must be placed in this context. Before we talk of socially useful schools and hospitals rather than bombs and bullets, we must acknowledge the basic fact of life that none of these comes without an environmental price tag. Nature serves up no 'free lunches', socially useful or not, and the signs are that her ability to provide has never been lower.

Individual rights place demands on other people, and there are limits to what we can expect others, or society as a whole, to provide. There can be no open-ended human rights. There is no blank cheque that promises the bearer 'to each according to his needs'. Popularly associated with Karl Marx, this theory has roots in Christianity. If put into practice literally, it would be a most eloquent suicide note. Individual entitlements cannot be separated from the ecology of human numbers and expectations. We live in a limited world, and this means limited rights.

The powerful and privileged have always used similar arguments to keep 'the rich man in his castle and the poor man at his gate'. It is not long since economic catastrophe was predicted if we stopped sending children down the mine, or freed the slaves. Violent repression was meted out to those who dared challenge the inequalities of a divided society. It is a situation little changed in most countries today. To this degree, the development of the concept of citizens' rights is one step forward in human thought.

CAMPAIGN FOR REAL RIGHTS

Commitment to human rights is a commitment to give individuals more control over their lives, and to remove human-made obstacles to personal fulfilment. Greens share this basic belief with many others. Where we differ is in judging the amount and kind of entitlements that a citizen receives against an ecological background. If this is not done (and the United Nations Declaration of Human Rights fails signally to do it with regard to the issues of population and migration) the dream of greater freedom is likely to turn sour.

If there are limits to the needs for which society can provide, their fair distribution is even more urgent. Social life contains many inequalities, in education, welfare provision, access to justice, and all the other essential components of equal opportunity. Limiting differentials between people is as essential as limiting economic growth and technological innovation. The realistic approach to human rights is to accept that their sum cannot endlessly expand, and therefore must be shared out as fairly as possible.

ME FIRST?

Individual rights must be balanced by responsibilities. Personal greed at the expense of others may be as old as humanity, but old social bonds have been severed, causing a vacuum into which has stepped a new individualism that claims rights but shuns responsibilities. Self-absorbed, it turns its back on the world at large and demands people's rights to 'do their own thing', be it dropping out of society or ruthlessly exploiting others. This subversion of social responsibility by egotism is a part of the rootless, mobile, anonymous mass society created by industrialism.

Many of our social problems — family breakdown, mental illness, drug addiction, crime, violence, indebtedness — are made worse by the personal dissatisfaction which industrialism encourages. This results from harnessing more and more human needs to the purchase of a constantly changing array of goods and services.

Human satisfactions are eroded in other ways. Some things have value just because few others own or use them. They range from a house in unspoilt surroundings, to uncongested roads and other facilities. A growth-based society — more people and more production — devalues such satisfactions, so their value is lost not just for the individual, but for everyone. Expansionism disrupts community bonds and displaces people. It fosters anti-social attitudes and behaviour, and all of the deadly sins except sloth, the one vice frowned upon in an expansionist culture. And in creating a bigger and more complex social system, industrial growth society not only breeds alienation, but actually heightens our collective vulnerability to disruption and breakdown.

The social costs of growth are most obvious in small stable communities which have suddenly experienced progress. They reach their most acute form, however, in the unstable cities where an increasing percentage of humanity is concentrated.

CRISIS IN THE WELFARE STATE

A whole variety of institutions have sprung up to meet the increased number of entitlements which citizens in the richer countries take for granted. Typical is the modern welfare state. Some of its origins were philanthropic, although others reflected the government's desire for a healthy and educated supply of people for the production process and the armed forces.

Today, post-war dreams of publicly funded services open to all have faded. The public welfare sector is declining both in quantity and quality, with more and more individuals jumping on board the 'lifeboats' of private schemes. Experience from the US, for example from health insurance schemes, suggests that these 'lifeboats' may in fact be full of holes.

Social inequalities and tensions often follow the privatization of social services. Many people might gain some benefit from these changes, but they foster the danger of an alienated under-class. Still, in most of the developed world, radical right-wing thinkers and politicians advocating policies such as the sale of public housing are in the ascendant. The whole idea of a welfare state has been made to seem out of date and inappropriate, and its traditional supporters appear unable to mount an effective defence. Instead they blame underfunding, or similarly evade the real problem; the Green diagnosis is radically different.

The industrial growth society has led to enormous social diffi-culties. These in turn require more management and more 'repair' work from institutions ranging from the police to the social services. Together these institutions constitute what American critic Hazel Henderson calls the 'entropy state', in which the cost of its social problems is becoming too expensive. More and more 'must be spent in mediating conflicts, controlling crime, footing the bill for all the social costs generated by the externalities of production and consumption, [and] providing ever more bureaucratic co-ordination'.

It is these costs that underlie the fiscal crisis of the welfare state. Until we change our way of living, they will continue to rise. No amount of extra funding will solve the problem. Indeed, the more money that is poured into the welfare state, especially for social security, the more resentment builds between the 'haves' and the 'have-nots', the latter being denigrated as idlers and scroungers living off the backs of the former.

This problem of rising costs and diminishing returns is not confined to those countries which have a comprehensive welfare system. The story of America's Health, Education and Welfare Office has been the same: the more it spent, the more it seemed to need. Kirkpatrick Sale's book *Human Scale* tells how, after millions of dollars were spent on housing and anti-poverty programmes, the South Bronx ended up in a far worse condition than before the Federal and New York City attempts to 'help' it.

THE CAREAUCRATS

Another negative aspect of both public and private welfare schemes is that they tend to create and encourage dependency. People become clients (rather than users) of professionals who, in effect, colonize aspects of human experience. The word client itself comes from the Latin for 'dependent'. We have experts on birth, childhood, youth, middle age, retirement and bereavement. As John McKnight says, 'the seven ages of man are replaced by the seven crises of man. The meaning of life is defined by a series of crises, and each attracts its own band of helpers and institutions'. Everything from job satisfaction to conflict resolution becomes the remit of one specialist or another. Professional organizations multiply, and admittance to them is gained by a parallel explosion in paper qualifications which certify an individual's competence in what, so often, human beings have always done reasonably successfully.

When 'service technologies' take over the field of human needs, people themselves tend to be disempowered. Traditional knowledge and customs and the skills of uncertified practitioners become suspect. Professions assume authority, diagnosing our needs and prescribing their remedies. They set the standards by which they are to be judged. It is in their joint interests to ensure maximum public funding and minimum public accountability.

Professionals need an increasing number of clients to 'serve'. Welfare professions respond to criticism by asserting 'that the problem is caused by lack of funds, citing high client-helper ratios, low salaries, poor technology and insufficient research ... the public must understand that what is needed is more of the same' (McKnight). New areas of growth are identified for expansion. 'If you are not sick, you are pre-sick and therefore need attention and check-ups.'

This ever-spreading 'clienthood' throughout life is a far cry from the notion of autonomous citizens freely choosing what help they think they need when they want it. In the writings of behavioural scientist B.F. Skinner, there is a genuine threat to freedom under the mask of professional care. Yet his vision of a totally manipulated utopia only takes to its logical conclusion the removal of self-reliance and self-mastery implicit in many of our welfare institutions.

DEFINING NEEDS

Taking their lead from the physical sciences, social experts tend to quantify human needs in an impersonal way. Everyone is said to require a specified amount of nutrients, floor space, medical time, tuition in a set number of subjects, years of employment and so on. This is reflected in the drab uniformity of much council housing, compulsory retirement ages, poor school meals, and the closure of small schools and cottage hospitals.

This ideology of basic needs also underlies many development programmes in the poorer countries. None would dispute the merit of bringing clean water to those who lack it. What is unacceptable is that many happily functioning communities are stereotyped as deficient just because they lack the right quantities of this or that service or facility.

Greens do not seek falsely to flatter individual potential: ignorance, malice and their like are too much a part of human reality. Yet we start from the assumption that people themselves are best able to judge what satisfies their needs, and that self-help and group initiative, where practicable, are more likely to provide satisfaction than bureaucracies, public or private. While many have gained from the services proffered by caring organizations, bureaucratization and professionalization often frustrate the very purposes these institutions claim to serve.

Welfare bureaucracies do not respond to human needs, but to demands. Demands are what the winners in our competitive society are best placed to make. So it is not surprising that the affluent and assertive sections of society often benefit the most from our welfare institutions, rather than the truly disadvantaged and deprived.

In many fields, discrimination against women and a general failure to pay due attention to their special needs remain rife. One obvious reason is that men take more than their share of top positions in institutions such as schools, hospitals and social services. But there are many general assumptions, particularly about the role of women as carers, which perpetuate the sexual segregation of who does what in society; and many traditional female roles, as midwives, for example, are grossly undervalued.

The increasing scale of services can also create remoteness and inflexibility. Some services in the field of mental health for example, are often sited many miles from the communities they are meant to serve. The welfare system is now so complicated that people can find it almost impossible to discover their entitlements. There are far more unclaimed benefits than illegal claims, though we have not seen many teams of investigators seeking out non-claimants!

The Green approach brings with it many implications. It requires access to relevant files and records, and a part in the design and operation of welfare systems. This is best achieved by small-scale and localized services. Users' committees offer a tool to make institutions more responsive to people's needs, as would 'advocates' for those not able effectively to assert themselves. It would also mean locating much more care in the community, placing the emphasis of public resources on services such as 'halfway house' accommodation, without which the move away from big institutions is likely only to increase the workload, on women in particular.

The most potent innovation would be the consolidation of the myriad welfare benefits and allowances into the basic income scheme. This would help separate livelihood from dependence on paid employment. People would thereby gain more free time in which to exercise more of their responsibilities to care for one another, which no bureaucracy can fully replace.

JUSTICE

The pursuit of justice has become confused with what is usually called law and order. Societies based on economic growth and centralized technologies require a high order of compliance from their citizens. As a result, on one front after another the rights of the individual citizen to be consulted and informed, to protest and resist, come under attack.

This obsession with law and order is a knee-jerk response to the serious problems of crime and anti-social behaviour, and we cannot simply blame poverty for such problems. Rising material affluence in the post-war years has not produced better citizens. Violent football hooligans often turn out to have jobs, and enough money to travel abroad to matches.

We do not pretend that the 'good old days' were free from such problems, yet in many ways matters have been made worse by today's rootless and competitive lifestyle. Industrialism has seriously undermined social structures such as the family and local community bonds, links which help to give individuals the security and identity necessary for respectful relationships. The boredom and futility of many jobs, and the emptiness of urban living, fuel the frustration exhibited by aggressive and disruptive individuals.

It is fashionable to denigrate social structures such as the family. Since most people live in families, it is not surprising that most violence is domestic violence. It is far more productive to focus instead upon the pressures that modern families have to bear, ranging from financial overcommitment to the problems of reconciling childcare and work.

Though it is naive exclusively to blame poverty, lack of resources amid general affluence creates a dangerously alienated underclass. The problems of its members are magnified by a welfare system which cannot cope with permanent deprivation. The survival strategies adopted by this expanding sub-culture make their own contribution to the incidence of petty crime. A system of basic citizen entitlement such as the basic income scheme would offset the traps of institutionalized poverty.

More police, more 'security' technology from camera surveillance or electronic tagging, and expanded prison, probation and welfare services are inadequate substitutes for what a healthy society can find within itself. They might, though expensively, help keep the lid on the problem, but will never remove its social roots. Essential rights and civil liberties are not safe in any society dominated by highly centralized and bureaucratic institutions. The citizens of most western countries enjoy freedoms lacking in those countries where repression is the rule, yet even here hard-won rights are being eroded. The crisis in the welfare state, in medical care, education and housing, is matched by attacks on accountability, freedom of information and the ability of citizens to organize themselves. Urgent legislation is needed to enshrine human rights in our constitution.

The European Convention of Human Rights and proposals such as those for a British Charter for Civil Liberties provide a sound starting point. Such legislation should enshrine the kind of 'amenity rights' discussed by economist E.J. Mishan, recognizing the absolute importance to human well-being of privacy, quietness, clean air and water.

Apart from the traditional safeguards against the arbitrary and oppressive exercise of power, a Green policy on justice would include the right of access to all personal data (and the right to correct wrong information); the right to stand for any election to public office; the right to vote in secrecy in all elections and ballots; the ability to initiate referenda by public demand on matters of public importance; and freedom of information.

Natural justice demands that these rights be balanced by responsibilities — to neighbours, to employees and employers, to society at large, to other species, and to the environment as a whole. Freedom of speech, for example, cannot be allowed to fan the flames of racial tensions. To permit it to do so is to deprive others of their rights.

15.
A ROOF OVER OUR HEADS

In housing, the key issues are (i) the right kind of buildings in the right places; and (ii) the provision of the means whereby people can afford to live in them.

These two issues raise questions about homelessness, slum districts and shanty towns, rent exploitation, crippling mortgage repayments, empty dwellings, houses in disrepair, building standards, optimum living space and suburban sprawl. Housing cannot be separated from a consideration of population, family structure, land ownership and planning.

Obviously population growth is a major influence on the provision of shelter, even of a basic kind. If there are homeless people now, in many countries there will be more tomorrow. Lack of livelihood forces people towards already congested centres, compounding the problems. The plight of those living on the streets of Calcutta is echoed by those under the railway arches of London.

Except in a few experimental initiatives, housing has barely begun to be understood as part of a socio-ecological system. The approach to house-building is short-life and resource-intensive, geared to growth-oriented economics. Without curbs on this kind of building the difficulties in the future will increase. The home-building of the '50s and '60s often created instant slums, which have had to be either demolished or expensively refurbished. As Fraser and Sutclife comment, 'having demolished slums which stood for a century, we constructed homes which lasted a decade'. The social utopia their designers promised failed to materialize, unlike the profits of those who built them.

Conventional critics of the failings of the private sector usually see the housing problem in terms of more units — hence the rhetoric of crash programmes of house-building. Unfortunately such large-scale plans do not respect local people or local environments.

Bad buildings are not the only failing in contemporary housing. The problems of mass public housing have been compounded by bureaucratic strangulation; an outstanding example of this has been the arbitrary use of building standards as a means of clearing whole communities, against the wishes of the inhabitants. Their preference to stay where they were and have public money spent on renovations, rather than on estates and tower blocks, is now generally accepted by those who once dismissed it.

The private sector causes its own problems. The property market has often produced inflated prices at one end of the country, while identical houses in other areas sell for far less. In time this will tear the social fabric apart. The roots of these distortions lie in the centripetal forces of our economic and political system, which draw decision-making, job and career opportunities, the arts and other aspects of life from the peripheral regions to the centre. Part of the housing solution must lie in general decentralization and far greater regional self-reliance.

Inflated house prices cannot be separated from the high cost of land. Land ownership brings the right to sell, which fuels the fires of speculation — to the detriment of the overall community. Green land policy is to dampen this process. Buildings themselves are another matter. Private ownership, whether by individuals or associations, is a major bulwark protecting the citizen against the abuse of state power. Also, the dividends of pride in appearance and maintenance accrue to all.

There will always be those who either want or need accommodation to rent rather than to buy. What matters is a rich diversity of choice within localities, providing of course that they are designed and constructed to proper standards of conservation.

There is such pressure to fulfil immediate needs that to advocate a policy of high-quality, long-life and energy-efficient building, which would mean high initial cost, is to fly in the face of present philosophy. We cannot afford the 'luxury', it claims, of such a policy. But to do otherwise is merely to repeat the mistakes that now disfigure our towns and cities. Minimal standards in materials, cost-cutting and a naive faith in the latest technology represent a false economy.

MATERIALS

Modern building, especially the building of offices and factories, is resource-intensive because of the energy and materials involved in the manufacture of materials such as concrete, steel and plastics for its construction, and also in its running costs. It builds in hazards for its users (this is especially true of synthetic materials). In terms of renewability and adaptability it is obviously unecological, unlike more traditional structures, which were usually made of natural materials available locally. In house construction the era of industrialization is proving short-lived, and a return to more traditional methods and materials is now evident. The problem is rather one of the materials that go into the houses once they are constructed; these are often hazardous in both manufacture and use. In addition the best forms of heat and sound insulation are seldom used, and practical advances in solar energy, water collection and sewage treatment are generally disregarded. Cost cutting raises doubt about the permanence of these buildings. The synthetic nature of today's culture is reflected in the synthetic attempts at 'character' on many new estates. Though an advance on the appalling standardization of recent decades, it is still far from the delights of the truly vernacular.

The most appropriate materials for construction and decoration are almost certainly those that come from close by, with the minimum of processing. The formulation and constant updating of building codes is critical. Already some architects and designers have proposed relevant guidelines. Malcolm Wells has listed the qualities of natural, undisturbed sites, and suggests that we assess building designs very carefully. We should encourage a sense of place, beauty, privacy and other more purely human considerations. Homes are to be lived in, not just machines for saving resources. With a holistic approach, standards for the design and construction of tomorrow's housing can satisfy all these needs.

Standards are necessary not only for new housing, but for all new building. Mechanisms must be created by which such standards are enforced and revised in the light of new information. Existing housing presents a massive challenge since so much of it was based, in its design and location, on the assumption of cheap energy. We need an extended programme of ecological upgrading. It may take many decades, but the optimum conversion or recycling of the present stock will bring direct benefits and many desirable spin-offs, not least in work creation. Wherever possible primary consideration must be given to refurbishment and renewal rather than clearance and rebuilding. Developments that go beyond renovation and infill in built-up areas would be given planning permission only as a last resort.

SKILL AND ACCESS

Green building policies would demand the highest craft skills. It is the cost of these skills that in part fuelled the switch to industrialized techniques. Since a Green economy would make resources more expensive than labour, there would be greater scope for human skills. Training would have to be overhauled to incorporate the best of skills, traditional and modern.

If humankind is going to solve the problems it faces over the coming decades, then it must make use of both old and new technologies that do not conflict with ecological principles. In a Green society, the opinions of future occupants would be sought by house designers and builders. To a degree this happens today, and encouragement would be given to extend the practice, particularly in housing where the user lacks 'client' status.

We must acknowledge that a Green housing policy incurs a greater initial cost, though this would be offset by low running costs and long life. However people choose to pay for their housing, it is vitally important that those on low incomes are part of this process.

Many people are bemused by the complexity of the present system of renting and owning homes. Sometimes financial institutions will only offer mortgages following stringent examination of applicants; at other times they seem to be treading on each other's toes to offer money for house purchase and improvement. Fluctuations in interest rates can open or close the door to home ownership, even though personal circumstances and property availability remain the same. Individual rights in rented property can be equally difficult to ascertain. Many people on the margins, such as the single homeless, are made to suffer particularly harshly.

Every individual has a fundamental right to decent shelter. Just as we need mixed communities of varied houses, where single-person flats, sheltered accommodation for the elderly and family homes are grouped together, so we also need a range of funding arrangements which take account of the new greening of architecture. These options must be such that they allow people of all incomes and status to be accommodated without fear of harassment or financial distress.

16.
SAFE AND SOUND

Physical and mental well-being is a basic measure of the true wealth of a people. Good living and good health march hand in hand. Yet life as it is lived in our industrial society systematically threatens both, undermining the achievements of modern medicine.

NATURAL DISASTER?

There is a general assault on our bodies from polluted air, water and food. Our factories and farms generate an unprecedented range of pollutants against which evolution has few defences. We contaminate our environment with air pollutants, pesticides, artificial fertilizers, raw sewage, radiation, noise, toxic trace metals and many other hazardous substances. Disaster movies such as *Towering Inferno* accurately reflect the fundamental dangers in many structures around us.

We have designed transport systems whose scale and speed can be spectacularly lethal, both directly through accidents and indirectly through pollution. We play God (or rather the Devil) with genetic engineering and germ warfare research. Through overpopulation and overcrowding we create environments ideal for epidemics. Our abuse of the environment produces back-lashes against our own well-being, ranging from minor complaints to respiratory ailments and terminal cancer. None will be significantly reduced until we clean up our physical environment.

The casualty toll from 'natural' disasters is as often as not a consequence of human disruptions of ecosystems. Avalanches, floods, forest fires, droughts and even earth tremors can all result from deforestation and other forms of environmental degradation. Technofixes for problems, such as flood control in river basins and sea walls along shorelines, tend in the long run to make such hazards worse, and to exact a higher price by encouraging the oversettling of unsafe areas. True natural disasters often have catastrophic effects because of negligence or inactivity by the authorities. This is particularly true in poorer countries, where the victims of occurrences such as volcano eruptions are often poor peasant families in rural areas.

EVERYDAY HAZARDS

A microcosm of environmental hazards is the workplace, where accidents and work-related illness take a heavy toll. The problems caused by strikes are quite trivial in comparison, yet preoccupy public attention. Official figures greatly under-estimate the death, maiming and general debilitation that result from the drive for greater and faster production, or from the use of dangerous materials and unsafe processes. Legislation on these, and on factors such as heating, lighting and ventilation, is reactive and piecemeal. Adequate enforcement is undermined by understaffed inspectorates. Profit is increased by cutting corners on safety standards and by covering up defects in products being marketed. Cutbacks, especially in the public sector, undermine proper training, checks and maintenance, inviting avoidable disasters.

We don't leave these problems behind at work. Our homes have become chemical cornucopias. We deluge our sinks, toilets, furniture, furnishings, plants, clothes and bodies with hazardous substances. We fit out our homes and wardrobes with inflammable artificial materials: devastating home fires are only the most visible sign of their risks. Even energy conservation has its dangers, such as the risk of internal air pollution in an over-insulated home.

THE FOOD FACTOR

Along with the hazards of our physical environment are the hazards of our diet. Industrialized food production causes problems, both by what it removes from and what it introduces into our diet, as well as by the excess of consumption that it encourages. Many well-researched books and TV programmes have recently increased awareness of the price paid for poor diet, from vague aches, pains and general debilitation to major killers such as cancer and heart disease. Their incidence has risen far more rapidly than increases in average lifespan, contradicting the claim that they are the consequence of more people living longer.

There is simply no need to eat ourselves so sick. Many ailments we take for granted are virtually unknown in people with diets different to those of the industrialized world. Happily, a few farmers and food manufacturers have continued to supply wholesome and tasty products free from the chemical cocktail of overprocessed 'junk' food. Some school meals services demonstrate that good cuisine and good health need not be restricted to conscientious households.

The failings of our diet stem from the way we produce and distribute our food. Consumers have become separated in time and place from the sources of their food. Local food production has largely been replaced by a global network, each corner specializing in a few crops. Nearer home, meanwhile, residues from pesticides and from hormones and antibiotics administered to 'battery' animals find their way into our food, so that nutritional quality declines as the intensity of production increases. As the corner shop is replaced by the hypermarket, foods travel vast distances along a lengthening distribution chain that is dependent on oil and electricity, and also chemical processes to retard natural ripening. Some of these chemical agents themselves have been implicated as primary health hazards.

The food manufacturing system works against good health in many ways. Costs are cut by replacing human skill and care with machines and chemicals. Cheap but nutritionally damaging ingredients such as fats, salt and sugar are exploited as basic raw materials, their blandness disguised by artificial colours, flavours and texture improvers. Prices can be raised by unnecessary processing of otherwise low-cost products. Mass production demands mass consumption, so new ways are sought to persuade us to eat more. Thus highly refined foods keep our stomachs hungry for more, while advertising tempts us with novel snacks between meals.

Bad diets flow from bad technologies and bad economics. They also reflect the way work is organized in our society. Many couples both go out to work, often travelling long distances. Time for proper food preparation and digestion is cut to the minimum. Sometimes the problem stems from ignorance, not least in cooking techniques.

Government policy on agricultural subsidies and school meals, regulations concerning food ingredients and labelling, and planning controls over retail outlets all exercise great influence. In general, the track record has been one of promoting or permitting what is unhealthy, from subsidising dairy produce to opening the doors to food irradiation, while at the same time protecting the food industry from public scrutiny.

Our diet is like a daily feast compared to that of preceding generations, or of those living in poor countries. It has evolved in a period when technology has been replacing human effort. Our bodies are those of a Stone-Age hunter/gatherer, yet we make our lives as inactive as possible. Fitness should be a natural by-product of a well organized society. Instead, expensive gymnasia have made it one more commodity to be sold to consumers who also buy all kinds of effort-replacing gadgets. Buildings and open spaces are planned as if walking itself were some kind of disease.

While not advocating back-breaking work, there is surely something wrong when resources are devoted to taking the effort out of switching TV channels or cleaning our teeth. Surface appearance, fads and gimmicks have become more important than our physiological needs in the design of artefacts we use daily. Seating and bedding, for example, often seem designed for some alien species with a different skeletal frame from us humans.

STRESS AND ADDICTION

Our society places unrelenting stress on its citizens. For all our material wealth, we endure anxiety, restlessness and general discontent. A profound lack of meaning pervades society, breeding a sense of pointlessness that is corrosive of mind and spirit. Industrial expansion has multiplied our worries in every corner of our lives: job security, promotion, debts, 'keeping up with the Joneses', dissatisfaction when our possessions become outdated or need expensive repair, and the loneliness and oppressiveness of our built environments. These concerns erode the stability of our family relationships, and undermine personal stability, calm and contentment.

The way we organize work underlies many social sources of illness as it does environmental ones. Some jobs simply place too many demands on people, precipitating nervous breakdowns and other signs of excessive stress. Others make people mere adjuncts to machines, numbing their minds with boring routine. Unemployment brings its own, well-documented worries, and there are many other ways in which individuals are made to feel outsiders, unwanted and undervalued by the structural inequalities that divide people. It is hardly surprising that many seek escape in drugs, and for some only suicide seems to offer relief.

Drug abuse might appear a purely self-inflicted wound, yet it reflects the depths of our alienation. Though the headlines concentrate on stories about hard drugs such as heroin, far worse dangers result from alcohol, tobacco and the array of medicines prescribed by doctors. Different cultures have, of course, been using drugs for centuries, and no one is compelled to take them. But what has changed is the power of those who manufacture them, and the intensity with which they are sold. These vested interests have sought to deny evidence of the ill health they cause, and to block legislation that might restrict the harm they cause to public well-being. The brewers, the cigarette manufacturers and the pharmaceutical corporations find powerful allies in those whose jobs and addictions depend on them. Faced with such opposition, governments have preferred to count the revenues they receive from what amounts to an organized drugging of society.

In farming, people often talk of the trend towards 'agribusiness'; in defence matters it is the 'military-industrial complex'. Similar developments have taken place in health, where what might be called 'medibusiness' binds drug and equipment manufacturers, insurance companies, and medical and managerial professional bodies. John McKnight points out that 'the expansion of the medical system is ... a primary means of providing income and markets disguised as help ... [It] requires the manufacture of need. As each need is created, citizens have an increased sense of deficiency and dependence.' Even reformers inside this system become trapped by its tunnel vision: 'Each reform ... represents a new opportunity for the medical system to expand its influence, scale and control.'

AGGRESSION AND HYPOCHONDRIA

Our culture's emphasis on 'masculine' values has serious consequences for health and safety. Decent regulations, warnings and education campaigns are often flouted by those — aggressive drivers, for example — who feel they need to demonstrate their virility and fearlessness even to their own and other people's cost. More systematically, one half of the population, women, have had their special needs ignored by male-dominated bureaucracies.

Our attitude to health reflects the failings of our culture. Sick animals will withdraw and recuperate, yet many adults demand to keep going at full speed, taking whatever pills suppress the warnings from their bodies. They expect perfect health; few civilizations have been so unwilling to integrate illness, ageing and death into the flow of life.

The cult of youth that seems to obsess Western culture reflects a lop-sided view. It refuses to accept the inevitable which, when it comes, is all the more painful. In the meantime, it creates a demand for any machine or drug that can maintain the illusion of permanent youth. People believe that with enough time, money and effort, every health problem has its remedy. Even 'alternative' medicine sometimes betrays an obsession with medication, pandering to what Dr Lewis Thomas has called 'healthy hypochondriacs'.

MEDICAL CARE

Last but not least of the threats to our well-being comes from the theory and practice of medical care itself. Professional medicine has been dominated by a perception of ill people as broken-down machinery, thought of not in terms of whole beings but of functioning parts. Investment has focused on greater specialization in surgery and drugs, to patch up the body when it breaks down. Resources are concentrated on the search for ever more sophisticated repair kits.

The mass production lines of industry are reflected in the centralization of treatment in enormous institutions. Their staffs are normally organized on hierarchical lines. Presiding over the profession is a powerful 'closed shop', always ready to defend its interests. The war which many of its members waged against the formation of the British National Health Service, for example, remains a monument to self-interest and group privilege. Today the system's 'stars' perform surgical feats of undoubted wonder, but which benefit only a handful of people, while programmes that could benefit millions are starved of funds.

Many of us have reason to be grateful for medical prowess in fields such as emergency care and infectious disease. Yet the doctors' technological power is generating as many problems as it answers. Overpopulation is just one example of a failure to judge medical innovation in terms of the moral, social and ecological consequences. Tireless effort is devoted to overcoming infertility, and prolonging the lives of the terminally ill or the mentally and physically incapacitated among our aged. The sanctity of life has become a device to avoid the fundamental issue of the quality of living. There are certainly no easy answers, but the refusal to make difficult choices is itself a choice that is storing up greater trouble for future generations.

Like industrial society as a whole, mechanistic medicine is becoming a victim of diminishing returns and negative side-effects. Addiction is not the only consequence of the over-reliance on drugs. Many people are in hospital because of the harmful effects of previous treatments. The excessive size of our hospitals works against the excellent care and attention given by medical staff. The unselfish commitment of nursing and ancillary workers is exploited as an excuse for intolerable wages and conditions of service. Their efforts may be frustrated by other aspects of 'hospitalization', such as hospital food, which often seems calculated to make the inmates more sick.

Partly through an obsession with gadgetry, medical training pays inadequate attention to vital ingredients of proper care like mutual respect, patience and an ability to listen. In general, health care has become a vast repair industry with an army of employees busy with expensive equipment and techniques. Its rising cost alone must force a fundamental re-examination of health policy.

As the *Black Report* on Britain's health care system showed, all of these problems are intensified by poverty. The poor suffer the worst pollution; they inhabit the dampest and most overcrowded housing; eat the worst food; receive the most run-down medical and welfare facilities; and generally have lifestyles which produce unacceptable inequalities in patterns of illness and mortality.

Expectations that the provision of health care would become cheaper as society's health improved were doomed to disappointment. Spending more on health is rather like providing more 'MASH' units near battlegrounds: good for patching up wounded soldiers, only to return them to the front. Debates over how much to spend on health services are ultimately a diversion. Particularly misleading are comparisons of the gross national product spent on health care. Countries such as Japan spend proportionally less than countries like Britain, yet their people are healthier. We have more doctors, more drugs and more hospitals than ever before. Specific shortages apart, multiplying their number will not bring a commensurate increase in public well-being.

Only a minority of patients, perhaps as few as 10 per cent, consulting their doctor will actually benefit from drugs or surgery. A similar number are suffering from something for which there is probably no treatment. For the rest, the best 'treatment' would be a change in their life circumstances. A switch to privatized hospitals and clinics is both irrelevant and dangerous, and in the long run this will probably cost society more as well as further tearing the fabric of social cohesion. It is medibusiness in its crudest form. Treatment should not depend on ability to pay. Providing a universal and genuine health service is a fundamental test of responsible relationships between people.

REAL HEALTH

Better policies begin with an adequate understanding of health, and the conditions that best maintain it. Rather than just the absence of illness, health should be perceived as all-round well-being, with accompanying resilience, the capacity to cope, and the ability to realize individual potential. Health does not exist in isolation, and should be seen as part of a total ecology of well-being which puts individuals in the context of their social and physical environment. The focus should therefore be upon correcting those personal actions, institutions or technologies which produce disease-creating imbalances.

A fundamental shift is needed to put prevention at the top of our priorities. The importance of preventative health care policies was shown by the improvements in public health achieved in Victorian and Edwardian times. It was not medical technology that brought about this development, but improvements in social conditions, especially in the standards of food, housing, water supply, sewage control and, significantly, the decline in the birth-rate. Today smear testing for cancer of the cervix has shown what can be achieved by an emphasis on primary care. Anti-smoking campaigns have probably saved more suffering and prevented more premature deaths than any other single initiative. Public education campaigns in Norway have led to dramatic successes in the reduction of heart disease, tooth decay and some cancers.

Green policies regarding pollution and environmental protection would work in conjunction with the encouragement of healthier lifestyles. Critical ecological zones such as watersheds would be protected, and standards set and enforced for air and water quality. Technological assessment procedures would make health and safety considerations central to the licensing of any new technology, process or product. The assumption would be that things may still go wrong, and therefore safe and speedy evacuation would be a fundamental requirement of both design and operation for everything from aeroplanes to leisure centres. Advice from the emergency services would help to strengthen present procedures. In some cases, such as in the industrial and safety inspectorates, the urgent need is simply for more staff. Money is better spent here than on, say, more chemists inventing new artificial flavours for food.

Other Green policies would improve the ecology of health. The switch to the soft energy path and Green transport policies would pay health dividends. So too would population stabilization and reduction, and the relief of urban congestion through the revival of rural communities.

The pressures of consumerism and of the fight for employment and promotion would be partially defused by the transition to a 'steady-state' economy, especially the basic income scheme (see p. 70), and by a great reduction in the amount and form of advertising. Freedom of information legislation would reveal hazards now kept from public view. In some cases, such as dangerous materials used in home furniture, it will take many years to rectify the short-sightedness of the past. Here all we can do is to launch intensive warning campaigns.

Decentralization and the promotion of 'human-scale' institutions would encourage a greater sense of control over the forces that affect our lives. Many Green policies would help to revive the extended family and local community as the basic building blocks of social life. Individual well-being would benefit from the resulting reduction in loneliness and dependence on institutional care.

HEALTH AND EDUCATION

The education system is an underused tool for improving both awareness of hazards and a deeper sense of personal responsibility. Health education should be central to the educational curriculum. General fitness depends just as much on the ability to relax as on the capacity for strenuous effort. The promotion of countryside rambles by children should be seen as an equally valid use of resources as high-tech sports halls. School meals could be used for teaching healthy eating habits as well as simply feeding children. Progress in sex education could include such issues as gender equality, the challenges of parenthood, and responsibilities regarding overpopulation.

NUTRITION

A healthy diet should be directly promoted by government. This is what happened in Britain during the Second World War, when the public seems to have been healthier than before or since. We would not, of course, want to recreate the circumstances and forced austerity of that period, but far from relaxing regulations as the food processing industry desires, policies need to be more rigorous and standards tighter. The fact that it has been necessary in recent years to withdraw several food additives emphasizes the need to require producers to demonstrate that innovations are harmless before they are introduced.

Agricultural policy should discourage the emphasis on meat and dairy produce. The German 'purity' laws on alcoholic products would be a model for regulations on the ingredients and processes of food manufacture. The public right to know could be extended by full declarations of a food's contents and, if necessary, processes, on publicly available registers kept by local government. Food labels should carry clear descriptions that do not mislead consumers concerning food value.

Food regulations and labelling would be handled by a ministry of food, responsible for all production, processing and retailing. Green policies to limit business size, especially by a turnover tax, would help to shift the balance back to local production for local needs.

SELF HELP

Complementing these individual actions to keep fit in mind and body, local communities would be encouraged to support general well-being through a network of health visitors, local clinics, first aid stations in public places, small nursing homes, sheltered accommodation and hospices. The Chinese system of 'barefoot doctors' shows that it is possible to demystify medicine and guide the community in health matters. The 1930s' British Pioneer Health Centre (the Peckham Experiment) demonstrated the value of empowering local people to help themselves.

MEDICAL FACILITIES

Many communities rue the loss of their small local hospitals, which only too often have been replaced by over-large and centralized facilities. Gains in specialist staff and equipment can be more than offset by a loss of accessibility and identity for patients and relatives alike, as well as by administrative headaches. We would therefore seek to reverse this trend. Wherever possible, medical help and advice would be dealt with at community level. General practitioners should develop into local experts, visiting the variety of centres in each locality to deal with matters beyond the scope of resident staff. As necessary, small but highly specialized units would serve large populations on a regional basis.

HEALTH RIGHTS AND RESPONSIBILITIES

Both healers and healed should have rights. The American tendency to pursue legal claims against doctors creates intolerable pressures and must be resisted, since successful treatment and recovery best take place in an atmosphere of trust. Equally, patients must not be seen as units being passed along a production line. All patients have a right to be valued in every respect as any healthy citizen.

Attitudes to AIDS and its victims have shown up many reprehensible aspects of human character. A modern equivalent of the scourges of the past, AIDS is exacerbated by the size and mobility of our modern population. Just as in former times, we must face the task of containment and possible cure. The situation could arise where private rights might have to be sacrificed for the public good. But it is a sick society that treats victims of a disease as sinners and outcasts.

Mainstream medical treatment involves violent intrusion upon mind and body. The success of many of these intrusions can be questioned in terms of their lasting benefits and side-effects, and Greens would promote proven 'alternative' therapies such as acupuncture and yoga.

The more spectacular feats of surgery are highly expensive and have equally costly support systems, draining the rest of health-care provision. We have reached a Catch-22 situation where we either use such technologies to save the few while downgrading the many, or allow individuals to suffer and die when the technology exists to save them. A balance must be found between individual and collective interests.

Many of the new medical developments are here to stay, but technical innovation must be subject to social control, in medicine just as much as in any field. Medical innovations would have to show demonstrable benefits in the broad social sense. Current and envisaged interference with human fertility and genetic make-up, for example, would be judged the height of irresponsibility, and be banned accordingly.

Finally, society must learn to acknowledge openly the inevitability of death, as many traditional societies have done. Heroic surgery in the name of the Hippocratic Oath must be balanced against the individual's right to die with dignity, care and comfort.

17.
SCHOOL'S OUT?

The present education system reflects the structures and practices of industrialism — hierarchy, conformity, competition, specialization, segregation and compartmentalization. What should be a necessary and helpful preparation for adult life is for many a dissatisfying experience, a conveyor belt to patterns of employment fast receding into history, never to return. This is felt among children, teachers and parents, and it provides fertile ground for politicians looking for bandwagons to ride.

There are many initiatives taking place which point to a better way. Yet as a whole the existing system is seriously failing, and some city schools seem to have passed the point of no return. Even higher education institutions are suffering a fundamental crisis of character and purpose.

BAD MARKS

Defenders of modern schooling often point to the rising number of exam passes. Even if this is true, what really matters is that the 'output' of schooling should be measured against the 'input'. Whether we judge by social behaviour, general knowledge, aesthetic and moral awareness or specific skills, the end result of so many years of compulsory schooling cannot justify the physical resources, time, money and effort it has consumed.

The need for overhaul is there to see. Classroom violence and vandalism on the one hand, and staff unrest and nervous break-downs on the other, are obvious signs. Classroom and play-ground sometimes breed brutalization rather than enlighten-ment. Actual teaching is only one of many roles that teachers are now expected to perform. Where there is unhappy family life the education system doubles up as a child-minding enterprise. Some parents resent school holidays not for the loss of education, but because they suddenly have to look after their own offspring.

Many initiatives outside the compulsory system receive inadequate attention. Playgroups, youth clubs, voluntary bodies and adult education can offer very rewarding experiences for their consumers. Yet too often they are separate from and inferior to the formal system, in status and funding.

The institutions of further and higher education have differ-ent problems from the inner city comprehensive schools. Patterns of privilege, of resource expenditure, of mechanistic, compart-mentalized and reductionist modes of thinking, dominate. It is little progress to boost student numbers if they are simply learning more and more about less and less, in areas and ways irrelevant to environmental and social problems. The very currency of the certificates that lie at the end of the educational paper chase is devalued, as more and more people possess them.

We are decidedly *for* study for its own sake; but this should not be confused with what has become an accelerating treadmill. In polytechnics and universities the functions of teaching and research have become badly confused. Students can appear a nuisance to academics, who are vying with each other to produce their research papers — more for career self-interest than to stimulate debate.

HALF-BAKED

Education is one area where there is no shortage of proposals for reform. Simply throwing more money at the problem is not the answer; we have being doing that for decades. Of course there are schools that need building work done and better resources, but the problem goes deeper than this. Plenty of educational institutions that are replete with all kinds of facilities achieve far less than much humbler and smaller places — including many village schools at risk of being closed.

Much spending goes on an expanding educational bureauc-racy, which can alienate those who have to live with the realities of the classroom. The education budget cannot keep on growing overall, and the knee jerk politics of 'no cuts' must not be allowed to get in the way of more fundamental reassessments.

Educational technofixes have offered a solution. First it was audio-visual aids, now it is the computer. These have their specific uses, but their contribution to the development of a fully-rounded individual is very limited. Indeed, in some ways the urge to introduce computing into all corners of the curriculum is likely to be downright harmful. The vital socialization of children, teaching them to work together, listen, be constructively self-assertive and so on, is unlikely to be encouraged if more and more time is spent in front of computer screens. Nor is individual creativity enhanced by working with computer programmes where all the key paramaters are already decided.

Worse, computerized number-crunching can suggest that life and the various disciplines through which we learn about it are reduced to what can be quantified. Qualities such as intuition, sensitivity and compassion, and a capacity to understand things as a whole and not just as a sum of parts, have no place in binary logic. The computer zombie is as much a threat to the society of the future as the uneducated lout.

Institutional rearrangements within an unchanged framework are unlikely to improve matters. It does not help to introduce a standardized curriculum based on what has already failed. Young people are not going to respond any better to subjects which they now spurn merely because central government says that they must study them. More testing will increase the meaningless cycle of preparation for the next test.

TRAINING TIME

Alongside this is the policy of reducing education to a matter of training. Real training, however, takes place not in fake simulations and superficial visits to workplaces, but over a period of time alongside someone already skilled in a craft or profession. Though the old apprenticeship system may have been overlong and exploitative, it was founded upon a sound principle of transferring skills from one generation to the next. Reviving the best of that tradition is an urgent need.

Some skills have been outdated by technological change, yet in many fields such as working with brick and wood, age-old skills are still at a premium. The shortage of skilled joiners and plumbers is one example. Moreover, in an ecological society that fosters repair and reuse, demand will increase. Automated systems cannot substitute for the human ingenuity and flexibility demanded in such work. But the bias of schooling is to equate manual work with menial work. Few initiatives for youth training address such problems.

Education is often seen as the acquisition of a set of marketable skills. Yes, we do need those skills, but human potential is only fully realized, both for the individual and for society, through a much broader range of experiences and understanding. There is no formal apprenticeship, for example, in wisdom or compassion. To base what is taught on a series of skills that can be measured and quantified debases what education should provide. Many human qualities and abilities cannot be confined within the framework of assessment. A narrowing of education to what is specifically 'useful' for today's economy and technology is inadequate. We must recognize the reality of change, and help young people to develop the ability to cope with it. This is far more likely to result from a broad range of educational experiences which enhance imagination, flexibility and vision.

PRIVATE EDUCATION

Some people want more private education, which would inevitably relegate the state system to a second-class service for those unable to pay. That the pupils of private schools often prosper in life reflects not on the kind of education provided, but on the social background and connections in which the private system is rooted. The personalities and limited horizons of some ex-private school children suggests that they may be victims rather than beneficiaries of privilege. To increase social segregation in education is quite unacceptable.

BIG IS NOT BEAUTIFUL

We have still not learned the lesson of the programme of closures and amalgamations which produced the mega-schools and colleges of today. The reasons why bigness is a blight in education have been well documented, as have the advantages of smaller institutions. We have created institutions whose managers require more effort and more resources than the teaching job they are meant to perform, and where individuals matter less and less.

PROGRESSIVE DOES NOT ALWAYS MEAN PROGRESS

In recent years there have been many attempts to give everyone the equal opportunity of good education.

Reforms which have tried to broaden and liberalize the content and method of education have failed for many reasons.

They often extend an already overlong curriculum and overload teachers and pupils with increased paperwork. Plans for 'profiling', negotiated between teacher and learner, take up scarce time and resources which can frequently be better deployed in other ways. Can we really assume that mature, professional adults and youngsters are equal negotiators?

THE DESCHOOLING TRAP

Some critics of modern education seem so influenced by its failings that they advocate throwing the baby out with the bathwater, by getting rid of all elements of compulsion. Instead of a planned public system, they envisage a web of associations and exchanges through which individuals would pursue their own education. Plans for educational 'vouchers' to be cashed in for tuition as and when desired would produce a similar pattern of learning. We should value the realization that people learn in many ways and from many sources, yet recognize that on the whole such changes would be socially retrogressive.

No change takes place in a social vacuum. To demolish existing structures would only widen social inequalities. Those who value education and have the funds available would ensure that their offspring did not suffer, while the children of less-motivated or less well-off parents would fall even further behind. For Greens, deschooling would also be to throw away existing resources.

Proper balance means a combination of freedom of choice *and* a degree of compulsion. It is a necessary part of life that we sometimes have to grit our teeth and work, rejecting our inclination to do things that might seem more instantly enjoyable or rewarding. Deschooling reflects the 'do your own thing' mentality which too often pays attention to self but not to society.

A CRISIS OF SCHOOLING OR A CRISIS OF SOCIETY?

The trouble with putting all the blame on what deschoolers call 'compulsory miseducation' is that it confuses symptoms with root causes. Problems in schooling are a reflection of problems in society; schools cannot be held responsible for inadequate parenting, devalued family life, the effect of changed ways of earning (or not earning) a living, or social inequality. Similarly, technological developments such as TV and home video seem to be lowering the boredom threshold and undermining the concentration of many children. Schools are victims rather than agents of such changes. Nevertheless more and more schooling has been accompanied by increased delinquency, drug abuse and other problems, and illiteracy is still widespread.

Deschoolers tend to underestimate what a reformed school system, in a reformed society, could achieve. On the other hand, mainstream educational reformers often overestimate what even the best system could attain. 'Limits to throughput' apply to educational processes as much as to anything else. The more institutionalized these processes become, the more the law of diminishing returns sets in. We must ask just what we want our children to know and value after so many hours in the classroom and laboratory.

We might begin to make real progress if we were to expect less in terms of quantity from education, and more in quality. If our children were not compelled to spend so much time in formal schooling, and were able to study fewer compulsory subjects, of a different form and content, this reduced goal would lead to a better real education.

GREEN LESSONS

Education is a key challenge in our current predicament. How can we socialize citizens, so they learn values and lead lifestyles appropriate to sustainability and conviviality, both between people and between people and planet? That question must be answered if we are to meet the classical notion of education as being the full development of the potential within an individual. The theory and practice of conservation should therefore inform all parts of the new curriculum. So too should the need to produce citizens aware of their rights *and* responsibilities, capable of full participation in the open and democratic structures of a conserver society.

A Green educational system would consider the following innovations:
- Less continuous time would have to be spent in the new formal system.
- Compulsory time in school would be shorter, both in total and for the school day. (Teachers and taught can only take in so much.)
- More time would be spent on activities that try to reunite the mental and the manual, equipping the individual with practical skills that boost individual self-reliance, whether in mechanics or music.
- Such activity would be partly based on real experiences and real problems, in school and in the neighbourhood; and partly on more didactic methods which can be quick and efficient ways of transferring knowledge and skills.

- The system would be based more on educational centres with a wide age spread. Individuals would spend most time with others of similar abilities and interests, but not necessarily of uniform age. Grouping individuals together because they were born in the same year has no intrinsic logic. A Green educational system would reflect the need to restore greater interaction between all age groups, as happens in the rest of human society. Formal divisions between primary, middle and secondary education could be replaced by a network of small neighbourhood education centres. These would be open all the year round, and would cater for a much more varied and flexible use.

- A fundamental principle is 'First Years First'. A child's first few years at school are decisive. Considering their importance in establishing skills and social awareness, today's primary schools are the poor relations of the entire education system. In a Green society reversing this imbalance would be given priority, even at the expense of slimming down elsewhere. There is an overriding need to establish the best teacher/ pupil ratios at this point, and not just later in the educational process. The incidence of inadequate parenting is a reality which society cannot ignore. It is here, in the primary sector rather than in an extension of compulsory school life, that resources should be concentrated.

- Part of such a reallocation of resources would provide for a web of playgroups and nursery education centres in each locality. Children would progress through part-time attendance into formal education.

- The 'conveyor belt', by which learners move *en masse* in year groups through a system of narrowing options, would be replaced by a flexible system. We suggest a network of units or modules through which individuals would find their own critical path. Such choice could not be limitless but, as far as practicable, individuals would proceed at their own pace and in their chosen disciplines. There would remain a minimum compulsory core built into the curriculum of required full-time education.

- The length of compulsory education could be defined either in terms of a minimum time period — perhaps ten years — or in the completion of a minimum number of key modules. Many people might object to both the earlier school-leaving age and the increased choice inside the system. They may fear that many would drop out too soon, and that this programme is tantamount to writing them off. In fact our aim is to switch resources to allow more people to 'drop back' into formal education if and when they feel the time is right. Forcing energetic young people to stay on unwillingly at school turns teaching into a job of control rather than education, which is damaging to all concerned.

- The freedom of choice would necessarily be restricted in the first years. This would be a 'foundation' period to ensure possession of the requisite skills for subsequent years. Within a short time there could be modules catering for those with distinctive needs. These may lead the child back to the mainstream, or in cases of severe learning difficulty might result in an extended series of special modules. The concept can be visualized as a critical path, involving some compulsory features which would diminish in number the further the individual progressed. Some studies would only be open to those who had successfully completed previous steps. Formal barriers to learning would be lowered further, by extending initiatives already seen, for example, in further and higher education. Courses which at present are separate entities, where a set group of students follow a given timetable, would become a permutation of modules. Any of these could be pursued by a variety of students. Beyond the foundation period, segregation by age would become less significant as individuals tailored their curriculum to their needs.

- The present institutional divisions would largely disappear. Methods of learning other than the traditional classroom would be more common. So-called distance learning is one possibility. More traditional teaching methods would be retained and enhanced by a reduction in non-academic stresses. The role of the teacher would be expanded to include guidance and tutoring. Far from being a burden, the emphasis on personal contact would enrich the educational experience for all concerned. Movement towards a more flexible and custom-made system would concentrate on helping students to find the right channel for their individual aspirations.

- Incorporating higher education into such plans poses special problems, because of the level of study and resources which many courses require. Initiatives such as Britain's Open University demonstrate the possibilities of avoiding élitist barriers. There would be devolution, from mega-institutions into many smaller establishments each offering a few special subjects, spread around the country. At certain points it would be desirable to build in gaps in full-time education to prevent people from becoming 'institutionalized' within the system. This would be particularly appropriate before access to the advanced modules which would replace the present system of higher education.

- A voucher scheme might be a useful way of giving a citizen an entitlement to periods of study at a higher level throughout a lifetime.
- Centres for pure research, for reflection and for discussion would have their own premises and resources. These should not be restricted to the cities, but situated wherever was most geographically appropriate.
- Learners would still need to receive feedback on their attainment levels, as would future employers and other interested parties. There can be no one dogma regarding assessment; what is appropriate to each educational experience will vary. We must, however, avoid the present trend towards formal overassessment, which endangers both the quantity and quality of teaching and learning.

CURRICULUM CONTENT

The new curriculum would contain both compulsory and optional elements. In the formal early years, the pattern would be similar to that of present primary schools, whose success is restricted by poor staff/pupil ratios, inadequate funding and pressure to follow fashions over the teaching of skills such as reading.

Once satisfactory progress has been registered at the foundation level, a programme of study would open out. Two fundamental areas (numeracy/logic and communications/study skills) would stand by themselves as a progression of compulsory modules, and also be integrated into other modules. Other core modules would cover parenting and health studies; civic studies (values, rights and responsibilities); the creative arts; ecolacy (how nature works, and its implications for people); and life skills (such as basic cookery and DIY).

Optional modules would cover whatever the locality, as well as the individual school, can provide, in both theoretical subjects and pure training. They would be pursued on site, not in school, if appropriate supervision could be arranged. An agreed programme of such studies would be followed during the period of compulsory education.

The network of modules would include ones available for those wanting reinforcement and revision, particularly in areas such as reading, writing and basic maths.

THE CONTROL OF EDUCATION

We would also seek to make decision-making in education more public. Rhetoric about 'parent power' often boils down to nothing more than a token involvement of a small, unrepresentative minority of parents. In the short term, it would be more useful to think of greater contact between parents and teachers. If we really want to remove the barriers at the school gate, home visits could be a legitimate part of a teacher's duties, with time allowed for them. Parents should also have access to all files kept on their children. In the longer run, a forum for parents to meet as a body would constitute a democratic means of electing delegates onto a school's governing body.

'Pupil' or 'student' power is a slogan less heard now. At one time people used to talk about schemes to put the evaluation of a particular educational experience into the hands of its 'consumers'. The dangers in this, not least of teachers 'playing to the gallery', outweigh the possible gains. Nevertheless, older students should be given more opportunity to provide feedback to those responsible for the content and methods of their courses.

Significant steps to greater democracy could be taken within the teaching body itself. At present it suffers excessive hierarchy, wide differentials and remote decision-making. As a starting point, those with the greatest teaching contact should have a majority on key committees in educational centres. More generally, responsibility for the broad outlines of education in a locality should rest firmly in the hands of the community and its elected representatives. There are examples of good practice from which we can draw lessons for the future. They point to the need to preserve a rich variety in our educational centres, in contrast to the inhibitions of centralized uniformity.

Like most rules, there is an exception. The private system, though doubtless contributing to variety, is an affront to equal opportunity and would have to be absorbed into the state system. There is no reason, however, why experimental schools should not continue, with support from the public purse.

A Green society would demand far-reaching changes in our education system, though the solution to many problems would depend on changes outside it. Parental involvement, for example, would otherwise remain little more than a pleasing idea. Progress depends both on a transformation of work roles, and on a reaffirmation of parenthood as a privilege bringing responsibilities that cannot be left to others.

18.
GOOD
NEIGHBOURS

Defence and foreign policy embrace the most dangerous expressions of our social structure and values. In the name of peace, governments prepare for and wage war. In the name of defence and co-operation, they carve up the world into political blocs whose lifeblood is the search for, and aggressive posturing towards, the 'enemy'. Military might is seen as an essential arm of foreign policy, which is defined in terms of national self-interest rather than congenial relations.

Jobs, profits and status depend on the production of increasingly expensive and sophisticated means of destruction. Though the profligacy of the developed world attracts most attention, poorer countries often squander an even higher proportion of their national spending upon weaponry. Encouraging all governments to do this is the most powerful lobby in the world, the arms manufacturers and dealers. The political-industrial-military complex has become a law unto itself in which the rivals feed off each other. As E.P. Thompson says, 'the show has grown bigger and bigger; the entrepreneurs have lost control of it, as it has thrown up its own managers, administrators, producers and a huge supporting cast; these have a direct interest in its continuance, in its enlargement. Whatever happens the show must go on.'

For this reason, so-called multilateral disarmament has produced few results. In Martin Ryle's words, 'those who argue that this kind of diplomacy is suddenly going to produce real progress ignore the blatant evidence of history, and must be convicted either of naivety or insincerity'.

BONE HEADS

This system, which Thompson calls 'exterminationism', thrives upon fantasies of physical power, whose roots go deep into our culture. The pathology of the 'defence through physical strength' mentality was voiced by Britain's socialist politician Aneurin Bevan when, dismissing what he called the 'infantile spasms' of nuclear disarmers, he said he would never 'walk naked' into the world's conference chambers.

Our entertainment media share the same fixations. From John Wayne to Sylvester Stallone, Hollywood has reflected machismo faith in violent solutions to human problems. Glossy magazines bring us glamorized accounts of wars in weekly instalments. Fact and fantasy have become most alarmingly blurred in the USA's Strategic Defence Initiative — or 'Star Wars' scheme. Pacifists, by contrast, have long been held up as objects of ridicule and scorn. To be gentle is to be soft and effeminate. Who, after all, wants sand kicked in their face?

A WORLD AT PERMANENT WAR

The combination of vested economic interests and violent cultural values has produced a situation where the world has never been such a dangerous place for ordinary citizens. Despite — or perhaps because of — the fact that governments are spending unprecedented amounts per head upon security, the individual has never been so unsafe. Since 1945, there has not been a single day when the world was free of war, and the number of people killed in the 140 or so 'post-war wars' has outnumbered the total dead of the Second World War. Regions such as Europe may have been at peace since the defeat of Nazi Germany, yet tensions derived from the power blocs that dominate the industrialized world have exploded in distant countries from Korea to Nicaragua. Local conflicts between e.g. Iraq and Iran have threatened to embroil people far beyond their borders.

Nuclear war, accidental or planned, could today obliterate entire peoples in minutes. From history, we know that arms races have produced only one result — war. The difference now is that it truly would be a war to end all wars, since the combination of radioactive poisoning, the cold of a 'nuclear winter', and the damage to the ozone layer would destroy the mechanisms by which societies recovered from past disasters. War is the ultimate pollutant.

THE WASTE ECONOMY

Preparations for war are costing us many of the things we most need to defend. The world spends more than 750 billion dollars a year on its military budgets, while all kinds of useful projects from clean water supply to the renovation of crumbling inner cities are neglected. The American military consumes some 10 per cent of the total US oil consumption. In 1978, the General Dynamics Corporation alone received $4,153,547,000 from the American taxpayer, money that could have been spent on halting the 'war' the USA is waging against Canada by means of acid rain.

The advantage for what economists such as Michael Kidron have called 'the permanent arms economy' is that it conflicts with few established business interests. Its very wastefulness provides an endless and lucrative sluice through which public money pours into private coffers. It is not just financial resources that are lost; we are also robbed of brain power, since over half the world's physical and engineering scientists work solely on military research.

FIGHTING FREEDOM

Democratic rights are threatened by the censorship, secrecy and surveillance that surround both individual military bases and arms factories, and the whole decision-making process of foreign and defence policy. The vigour with which the public is kept in the dark is matched only by the vigour with which the different military and secret services fight each other for resources. From the sinking of the *Rainbow Warrior* to the repression of Soviet dissidents, espionage agencies have proved a more persistent threat to civil liberties than any external enemy. As Ruth Brandon put it, 'however paranoid you are, you're probably right'.

At the head of the vast defence establishments is a small, secret and powerful clique of policy makers. Globally it has been estimated that there are some 800 people, virtually all men, who on their own initiatives take the key decisions over weapons procurements and military doctrine. Protected from public scrutiny, many defence bureaucracies are monumentally ineffective and inefficient.

Political sovereignty is another value that is violated in the name of security. Countries like Britain act as an aircraft carrier for the American air force. Episodes such as the assault on Libya demonstrate the state of subservient clienthood that can await nations who host foreign bases.

MUTUAL RESPONSE

Aggressive posturing threatens peace itself. Far from preserving peace, any policy of deterrence is intrinsically unstable, triggering off a cycle of action and reaction by rival powers. The arms race is its inevitable expression. The participants long ago passed the point where they could wipe each other out. They can now repeat the job many times over, yet still the race goes on. No sooner is one agreement struck than the search starts for new forms of unilateral rearmament. Hardly had the ink dried on promises to remove 4 per cent of the world's nuclear arsenals than NATO was planning new generations of nuclear-capable aircraft and sea-launched Cruise missiles, which the Warsaw Pact powers will try to copy and overtake.

Once one state possesses a certain weapon, the door is opened to its spread to other countries, undermining any security which possession might have brought to its first owner. Nuclear proliferation will put many more fingers on the trigger by the end of the century, and multiply all the current instabilities and uncertainties. It is hypocrisy for any country to decry this process while retaining possession of nuclear weapons. If it is true, for example, that British warships took such weaponry to the Falklands war zone, any future Argentinian government could claim it is legitimate to develop identical capabilities.

BLIND MAN'S BUFF

Defence and foreign policies produce tensions that could tip over into catastrophe at any time, for we are gambling our peace on a system of bluff and counter-bluff. During the Cuban missile crisis, the gamblers got it right and life went on. But the system only has to fail once. It brooks no misjudgment and no acts of irrationality.

The spread of miniaturized nuclear weapons is undermining trust-building processes such as verification, and is creating new scope for miscalculation. Studies by writers such as Norman Dixon and Geoffrey Regan of political and military incompetence and error in past decisions afford little confidence for the future. It is as though we guard our future by pointing a pistol to our heads, and saying to aggressors, real or imaginary, 'stop or I'll squeeze the trigger'.

This historical novelty makes redundant selective examples torn from history about how military strength might, for example, have deterred Hitler in the 1930s. The past simply did not contain the dangers of the present.

FINGERS OFF THE TRIGGER

American economist Kenneth Boulding identifies the key conflict: it is 'between the human race itself and its national defence organizations which threaten to destroy it ... Any realistic appraisal of the world situation would come to the conclusion that the national state, no matter what it is or how virtuous it is, should not be defended, because its defence can only lead to the destruction of us all.' This is a moral indictment of any firm or university laboratory involved in arms research: 'Anybody who is employed by or works for a national defence of the human race should be utterly ashamed of what they are doing.'

The extremism of Professor Boulding's analysis is the only realistic response to the dangers of deterrence and the arms race. Greens share his stance not as pacifists (though we admire their stance), but because the technology of modern war leaves no alternative. Boulding stakes out a position with many risks, but whatever the risks, they are less than those built into the present situation and the ineffective attempts to reform it.

NUCLEAR DISARMAMENT: THE ONLY HOPE

Under no circumstances could the consequences of unleashing today's nuclear arsenals ever be justified. No responsible government could therefore even threaten such an act. There is no point in possessing something which a sane person could never use. To uphold the theories of deterrence and the balance of terror is to underwrite the possibility of burning alive millions of innocent people, or poisoning them with radioactivity. The alternative, inescapable for those who value life on earth, is to renounce nuclear weapons and withdraw from any alliances whose military doctrine rests upon using them.

That in itself is not enough. Modern conventional weapons are becoming so devastating that they too are eroding the notion of a winnable war. It is perfectly possible that superpower strategists might themselves soon be advocating an abandonment of nuclear defence, in favour of much cheaper but equally 'efficient' alternatives in the field of chemical and biological warfare. A war waged, for example, to 'save' Western Germany from Soviet incursions by use of modern conventional weaponry alone would leave nothing worth saving, such has been the escalation in firepower. The Vietnam War was not worth its cost from any point of view. Alternative defence strategies must be more radical than a simple shift to conventional bombers, tanks and artillery.

POLITICAL PREDATORS

The sheer size of rival nation-states makes the situation especially dangerous. People sometimes justify these states and their defence policies by pointing to all the little wars that used to plague the German principalities or the Balkans. But in such circumstances their small size was a virtue, not a vice. In the Balkans, the serious problems started when the superstates of the later nineteenth century led by the Kaiser, the Tsar and the Emperor of Austro-Hungary became involved in local affairs, ultimately triggering the First World War. Today peoples from Nicaragua to Eritrea are paying the price for superpower machinations. Local 'bush wars' now sow the seeds of conflict that can spread way beyond their boundaries.

Using the researches of the Boston Study Group, Amory and Hunter Lovins have shown that some 97 per cent of the US military budget goes not to defend American citizens from any conceivable threat, but 'for general-purpose forces to project American power into other people's disputes in other countries'. The situation is similar in other powerful states. In an increasingly competitive world, what is really at stake are markets, investment outlets and sources of raw materials. The declining years of the industrial growth society threaten to give such pressures for conflict ever more explosive force.

EMPIRES RISE ... AND FALL

We need not be mesmerized by the seemingly unbreakable stranglehold which the existing superpowers exert over human destinies. As Kenneth Boulding comments, 'empires have corrupted and impoverished the imperial power, simply because threat is a very poor way of getting rich as compared with production and exchange'. From American budgetary problems to the explosive ethnic tensions within the Soviet empire, there are many signs that their ascendancy is coming to an end. A window of opportunity is opening for an escape from the world of the big power blocs, but it will require a prolonged struggle against those who, for example, aspire to see a United Europe replace the present nation states.

TOWARDS A SAFER WORLD

Amory Lovins and Hunter Lovins define 'real security' as a situation where 'we strive to make our neighbours feel more secure, not less — whether on the scale of the village or the globe'. It is, in other words, the opposite of the goal of current defence and foreign policies. Future safety depends upon steps that will get us all off the precarious tightrope on which humanity is currently perched.

Any government only has the power to change its own policies, and the best contribution we can make to the promotion of general peace is to put our own house in order. The force of example has produced more lasting change in the world than the force of threat. For this reason British Greens seek to ban British nuclear, chemical and biological weapons. Foreign bases and visits by foreign nuclear forces would be terminated. Related research centres such as Porton Down would be closed. The charade of nuclear civil defence would cease. The Defence Sales Organization would be disbanded, and no more military shows and parades held.

Amory and Hunter Lovins have described the kind of defence posture a Green government would promote. It 'would make one's national territory impossibly disagreeable for anyone else to occupy. Such a purely defensive military posture is cheap; threatens nobody; cannot be perverted into an instrument of oppression; and can even guard against tyranny at home.' Countries such as Sweden, Switzerland and Yugoslavia provide examples of the kind of 'hedgehog' defence principle whose relevance to our needs should be explored. We should never forget that, as Kenneth Boulding argues, 'a well-managed defeat is often much more productive than a costly victory'.

Withdrawal from existing military alliances would be necessary. Commitment to people over whose actions we have no control always carries risks, but never so much as when they are armed with nuclear weapons. Mutually beneficial links are usually to be found between equals, not between big powers and their clients. A position of non-alignment would guide future foreign policy. Militarists will dismiss this by saying that 'we want to stop the world and get off'. In fact, it is a sensible policy to distance ourselves from postures that threaten war, and to seek more constructive relationships wherever we can find them.

The Green energy policy of closing down nuclear energy facilities will help to sever the intrinsic link with the nuclear weapons programme. While discoveries can never be 'uninvented', their application can be made easier or harder. By shutting down the civil nuclear programme, we would be adding at least one barrier to preparations for war.

THE BREAKDOWN OF SUPERSTATES

A Green government should apply decentralist principles to itself and, by breaking the state into a confederation of regions, set a positive example to other countries. In many regions, separatist movements already demonstrate the artificiality of the arbitrary and enforced unions on which many states are based. The peaceful separation of Norway from Sweden at the beginning of the century stands as a model of how this can be done to the general benefit of those citizens concerned.

FISSION NOT FUSION

A Green government in Britain would come into conflict with the EEC, since the basic principles of that organization, especially the idea of a common market, are profoundly anti-ecological. Though it has set some progressive standards over pollution and citizen's rights, the intrinsic anomaly of having the same policies for such different cultural and geographical areas as Sicily and Northern Scotland makes the EEC an organization with no long-term role in a decentralized Europe of regions. EEC-sponsored centralization and standardization must be replaced by a diversity based on what is locally, environmentally and socially appropriate, keeping decision-making as close as possible to those most affected by the decisions.

ONE WORLD?

The United Nations and its agencies seem to oscillate between impotence, and the dissemination of the often harmful models and practices of the overdeveloped states to their less developed neighbours. The anachronistic power structure of the Security Council of the United Nations institutionalizes the worst features of the world political order. In many ways, the concept of 'one world' is a myth, albeit sometimes a useful one. Few problems are truly global. Most are local in both origin and solution. Rather than pretending that the United Nations can be something it never could nor should be, we would seek to influence it towards the more modest but meaningful role of an international conciliation service.

ECO-PEACE

The kind of conserver society discussed in this book is an essential feature of any policy for real security. Water pollution and soil erosion are two examples of aggression against resources we vitally need. All else is secondary to the defence of environmental integrity.

Increased self-reliance makes us less vulnerable to external events. Fred Trainer shows how most disarmers 'miss the point ... A peaceful world order cannot be achieved without fundamental change to values and social structures, a change that does not generate such high *per capita* rates of resource use ... To endorse the impossibly resource-hungry levels of affluence typical of the developed countries ... is to commit oneself to the increasing exercise of force in order to secure the resources necessary to sustain that affluence ... Unless the disarmament movement is grounded on basic "limits to growth" insights it is in effect no more than a plea to have our inescapable imperialist conflicts fought with conventional rather than nuclear weapons.'

Countries such as Japan, which in the 1970s imported 98 per cent of its iron ore, 100 per cent of its aluminium and nickel, and 88 per cent of all energy requirements, sow within themselves the seeds of expansionism and aggression. Only by shifting to a society that reduces such consumption can we defuse these explosive tensions. Fritz Schumacher summed up the roots of such tensions in our expansionist economy and materialistic culture: 'The foundations of peace cannot be laid by universal prosperity in the modern sense, because such prosperity, if attainable at all, is attainable only by cultivating such drives of human nature as greed and envy, which destroy the intelligence, happiness, serenity, and thereby the peacefulness of man ... The cultivation and expansion of needs is the antithesis of wisdom. It is also the antithesis of freedom and peace. Only by a reduction of needs can one promote a genuine reduction in those tensions which are the ultimate causes of strife and war.'

COMING DOWN TO EARTH

The UK Green standpoint on defence and foreign policy, applicable also to the related issues of trade, aid and migration, reflects one central perception. We live on a small, overcrowded island that has been taking upon itself roles — political, military, financial — that are well beyond its means. Many of them have their roots in the fact that we were the first country to industrialize. However institutions and ideas live on long after the circumstances that supported them have disappeared.

The Falklands War was a painful reminder of how imperial vanities survive — on both sides. Readjustment is inevitable. Britain can however make one last act on the world stage, by being the first country to set an example of how to make the transition from industrialism to a truly secure and satisfying society. Dorothy L. Sayers has commented that war is a judgment that overtakes societies: 'they happen when wrong ways of thinking and living bring about intolerable situations'. Only Green policies are equipped fully to change those 'wrong ways'.

19.
THE GLOBAL POVERTY TRAP

Over one billion people are living in conditions of desperate poverty. They lack adequate food, clean water and sufficient fuel. Measured by every indicator of well-being — life expectancy, literacy, personal income — they constitute a global underclass; and their numbers are fast growing. The victims of famine and civil war may grab the news headlines, but there are many more still trying to scratch a living in the shanty towns or on the barren marginal lands across Latin America, South Asia and Africa.

In the West, every section of society is tremendously privileged in comparison with the world's poor. The response to charity initiatives like Band Aid suggests that many individuals want action against the horrors typified by Ethiopia. Yet the record of government after government has been at best one of token and belated gestures. Money continues to be spent on arms while the world's poor suffer.

AID FOR WHOM?

Aid is not only insufficient — meagre crumbs from the rich countries' tables — much of it is also in the form of loans that have crippled the recipients with a burden of debt. Interest charges and debt repayments are undermining the economies of poor countries and threatening the very foundations of the world monetary system.

In 1983, developing countries paid Western banks $21 billion in debt servicing. Only measures like loan write-offs, elaborate rescheduling and greater austerity within the debtor nations are postponing a wave of defaults which could herald a financial crisis far worse than anything seen so far. Many of the imposed belt-tightening measures are at the expense of the poorest; the International Monetary Fund's stabilization plan for Costa Rica, for example, led to a doubling of the number of children suffering from severe malnutrition within one year.

Aid is often tied to the purchase of goods from the donor country. The £70 million helicopter deal struck between the British and Indian governments, for example, was a form of aid to the ailing firm of Westland, not the poor people of India. More generally, aid is being given to projects that serve the interests of both the rich classes in Third World countries' and the industrialized world as a whole.

The political use of aid is well-documented. Around the world various regimes are propped up to serve the military and economic interests of the rich countries. For example, Israel, central to Western interests in the Middle East, has received more aid than any other country, while 70 per cent of American aid to Central America is for 'security purposes'. Furthermore, when local governments have tried to initiate internal reforms, aid is suddenly cut off if they do not fall back into line.

However the roots of world poverty go much deeper than the shortcomings of different aid packages. The major political parties argue continually over who has given the most money, yet none of them seeks to tackle the basic issue — the relationship between the rich and the poor countries.

COLONIALISM AND AFTER

Beyond widespread internal poverty, the poor countries have one characteristic in common — nearly all of them have at one time been European colonies. Sophisticated communications and military technology enabled Britain, France and other powers to subjugate large parts of the world. The consequences are still with us today. Cultural and environmental factors were ignored as the new rulers marked out the territories. They created artificial political entities which, after independence, have been plagued by discord and civil war.

Many of the conquered lands had seen civilizations older and more sophisticated than those of their new rulers. The impact of colonialism was disastrous: the frequency of famines in India under the British Raj, for example, increased sixfold. The social and economic structures of the colonies were tailored to suit the requirements of Europe. Raw materials flowed from mines and plantations via new roads, railways and ports to the heartland of the Empire.

Independence has brought little change for the poor of these former colonies. Government tariffs, quotas and the workings of world commodity markets ensure that today's trade still favours the rich. The profits from commodities like tea and coffee go not to those who planted and picked them but to plantation owners, government bureaucrats, traders, brokers, shippers, retailers and shareholders. Cheap labour, low prices for Third World produce, profits taken back to the company headquarters in the developed world, the evasion of taxes through transfer pricing, are some aspects of a system that drains between 50 and 100 billion dollars from the Third World each year.

The role of transnational corporations is crucial in this system. They control a third of world production and dominate trade in many commodities. Unilever, for example, the world's largest food conglomerate, has a turnover greater than the GNP of 25 African states; 80 per cent of the oil trade is controlled by just seven companies; the UK-based Consolidated Gold Fields has been making pre-tax profits of around £115 million a year based on the starvation wages and hazardous working conditions of black South African miners.

Private profiteering is, however, only one part of the overall picture. The lifestyles of all classes in the industrialized world are maintained by this international system of investment and trade. After a detailed review of the evidence, F.E. Trainer has concluded that 'most of the resources used within the global economy are flowing into rich countries from poor countries and remaining among rich countries'. America gets around half its supply of industrial materials from the Third World; the figure for fruit and vegetables is as high as 75 per cent. Many of those at the Band Aid concerts would have been wearing clothes made from Ethiopian cotton while chewing peanuts from the Sahel. Many hamburgers eaten that night could have come from new ranches carved out of irreplaceable rain forests in Amazonia or the vulnerable grasslands of Botswana.

It has been estimated that people in the rich countries are using 40 million acres of Third World land for their tea, coffee and cocoa. Whole islands in South-East Asia are being deforested by Japan to provide woodchip for its industries. In the same region, the expansion of the 'brothel holiday' industry is adding new dimensions to the exploitation of that region.

We in the West not only lead lives based on a flow of cheap resources from the poor countries, but are also using the Third World to do our 'dirty work' and take our wastes. Many polluting industries have relocated themselves in countries like Brazil, to escape health and safety regulations and trade unionism. In addition, the hazardous by-products of our industries now constitute a growing export to the Third World. A Norwegian-Guinean company, for example, has been dumping thousands of tonnnes of dangerous toxic wastes in West Africa.

Hospitals and other institutions benefit from a brain drain from poor to rich countries. Jan Tinbergen estimates that Third World 'wealth' lost in migration of talented personnel to rich countries from 1960 to 1972 was greater than the value of all aid.

SELF-INFLICTED WOUNDS

Global poverty is, however, not just the fault of developed countries. Regimes across the Third World have been active accomplices in the maldevelopment of their lands. Terms such as 'the Third World' or the more recent label 'the South' disguise the enormous inequalities within these countries. Local élites (landowners, business and professional people) are often behind military dictatorships or one-party states. In Central America 10 per cent of landowners control 80 per cent of the farmland.

These powerful social groups are in many ways today's new internationalists. Thoroughly Westernized, they have little in common with the ordinary people of their countries. Sometimes local rulers have even diverted development funds into their own bank accounts. The Philippines paid dearly for the rule of the Marcos family, personal friends of many leading politicians in the West. Many of these regimes have heavily armed forces to repress internal opposition to their misrule, further draining national wealth. On average, poor countries are spending 40 dollars per head on arms compared to only 27 dollars on education. Local wars and aggression from more powerful neighbours make the situation worse.

Many Third World countries have sought, in the name of modernization, to emulate the industrialized world. The devastating environmental and social impact on these countries of massive schemes financed by institutions like the World Bank — vast ranches, superdams — has been well-documented. In addition, the resettlement programme on the outer islands of Indonesia and the Brazilian exploitation of Amazonia show how readily Third World governments can rival the worst deeds of colonialism. Tribal peoples and rural villagers in the way of 'progress' are crushed as ruthlessly as were the Red Indians of North America in the nineteenth century. Indonesia, for example, has killed over 100,000 people in East Timor. Opposition, however, is silenced: President Nasser was quick to lock up those Egyptians who accurately predicted that the Aswan Dam would be a disaster.

Third World governments have set their sights on national airlines, high technology city hospitals, motorways, nuclear power plants, office and apartment blocks, smart hotels, and all the other paraphernalia of industrialized society. The pattern is the same in agriculture. In Tanzania the Nyerere government, with Canadian support, is promoting Western-style wheat growing. Farmers will be dependent on high-cost imports of the necessary fertilizers, pesticides and machinery while subject to the vagaries of the grain trade. Previously self-reliant communities like Ladakh in the Himalayas are being made dependent on external forces in the pursuit of 'development'.

The local roots of Third World problems are also cultural. The surge of human numbers can only produce catastrophe as many Third World governments, especially the Chinese, have realized. Yet Malaysia has said it wants its population to increase by 400 per cent to 70 million during the next century.

Even with the wastefulness of our Western diets, 80 per cent of the increase in the demand for food is still attributable to the need to feed more people. Other problems are also exacerbated by population growth. Many cities are bursting at the seams — the result not only of the huge migration from rural areas but increasingly of internal growth too. São Paulo is now so big that it consumes nearly half of Brazil's electricity; in Egypt, Alexandria's sewers, built to serve one million people, have been overwhelmed by four times that number. By the turn of the century, the Third World will be seeking an additional 676 million jobs for its workforce. This eruption in human numbers is taking place in the same environments that contain the richest reservoirs of animal and plant life and whose forests are crucial for the stability of global climatic patterns.

The association of poverty with large families is well known. Yet large families are also the product of strongly male-dominated cultures where large numbers of offspring, especially boys, are considered desirable. Religions as varied as Roman Catholicism, Rastafarianism and Islam have also played their part in encouraging child-bearing in societies increasingly unable to cope with it. Opposition to family planning has been widespread: left-wing leaders like Fidel Castro have denounced it as an imperialist plot. Women are made to suffer in other ways, too, like forced female circumcision which affects some 74 million girls each year.

There is a great deal to value and to learn from the cultures of the Third World. Yet we in the rich West do harm if we remain silent about the forces within the Third World that encourage environmental destruction, poverty and population growth. There are many who see so-called progressive regimes through rose-tinted spectacles. This is especially true of China, whose enthusiasm for superdams and nuclear power plants, and whose brutal role in the affairs of Tibet and South-East Asia are tacitly ignored by left-wing apologists. China is now the world's fifth largest arms trader and was simultaneously selling arms to warring Iraq and Iran. Ethiopia, too, has escaped severe condemnation. More vigorous criticism of the Ethiopian regime's agricultural and settlement policies, and its repression of regionalist movements might have forced it to change course and spare its people yet more suffering.

THE PROBLEM OF DEVELOPMENT

There have been economic success stories in the postwar history of the Third World, but these have been the exception rather than the rule. Some have been city states and small islands without a vast peasantry. Others sat on large oilfields which provided a passport to wealth. China is the outstanding example of a country that managed to feed its people by its own efforts, though at considerable cost: political regimentation and extensive environmental damage.

Beneath the glitter of the economic 'miracles' like South Korea there is often an uglier reality. Workers in Korean factories work the longest hours and endure the most hazardous conditions in the industrialized world. In one high-tech electronics firm in Sri Lanka, it was found that 80 per cent of the women workers suffered from chronic conjunctivitis while 44 per cent had become nearsighted.

More generally, both poverty and environmental destruction are in fact now worse after decades of development. In Latin America, *per capita* income has fallen by 9 per cent since 1980. Any wealth generated in the new factories of Brazil and other rapidly industrializing lands has not trickled down to the mass of people. It has simply stayed in the hands of the rich and powerful who spend it on more luxuries.

Far from creating jobs, industrialization, especially agricultural mechanization, has intensified the basic problem. The transformation of Third World agriculture through high-yielding hybrids has not only created ecological havoc but also driven out small farmers, thus increasing poverty. The big farmers have benefited most from a form of agriculture dependent on expensive fertilizers, irrigation and other inputs. Evidence collected by researchers from Canada's Energy Probe Foundation shows that rural electrification has not improved the well-being of most people, by encouraging the use of machines and displacing human labour.

The environmental costs of development have been colossal. Tropical forests, which contain around half of all plant and animal species, are being destroyed at such a rate that little will remain in 50 years' time. The traditional slash-and-burn form of cultivation is now being practised on such a scale that the forests can no longer cope. India's forests have decreased by 50 per cent since independence. Deserts equalling the size of Europe have been created across the world by development schemes, especially the extension of water-dependent mechanized farming and increases in herd sizes.

Industrial workers, local residents and the environment as a whole are suffering from dangerous pollution. Other environmental backlashes include droughts, floods and landslides. The deaths of well over 300 Brazilians in a torrent of mud on the edges of Rio de Janeiro in early 1988 were not caused by an 'act of God' but by deforestation.

The development process has treated Third World countries as no more than a reservoir of raw materials. Far from deriving any comparative advantage from such specialization, their economies have become more unstable. Apart from the environmental hazards of increased monoculture and the wastefulness of transporting produce from one side of the planet to the other, it has made producer countries even more vulnerable to sudden falls in commodity prices. Speculation on world commodity markets, synthetic substitutions for natural materials, more efficient production processes, changes in fashion or a slowdown in Western economies can all spell ruin for countries trapped in this form of dependency. At the same time poor countries are burdened by the cost of the high-technology goods they import from the developed world.

There has recently been a rising chorus of demands for a new economic order. Inside the industrialized countries, too, pressure groups campaigning for global equity have multiplied. However, many of the reforms now being discussed fail to face up to the radical changes needed in the pattern of international political and economic relationships.

READJUSTMENTS ARE NOT ENOUGH

Some argue that the rich countries should pay more for what they import from their poorer neighbours. 'Fair trade' has become a popular slogan. Yet relations between unequals are always likely to work in favour of the strong. Higher prices would still not alter the basic structures of dependence nor remedy the ecological unsustainability of these patterns of trade. Any increase in the money paid for Third World produce would go to local ruling classes. Significantly, as John Madeley observed, people in the villages of Tanzania and Uganda were better fed when foreign trade was depressed because the villagers kept what they had grown and ate it themselves.

We should not be trying to bring more sections of global society into the market economy, an approach typified by the work of the American organization Women's World Banking (WWB). Its president Michaela Walsh publicly cites as an example of successful entrepreneurship a group of African women that WWB financed to grow tobacco. Yet, apart from the health hazards of smoking, this plant destroys the soil, and firewood for tobacco curing is responsible for massive deforestation. Initiatives like this ensnare people in a cycle of human and environmental destruction.

We have to re-examine the whole philosophy on which such policies are based. Even if we could purge the system of its more exploitative features, its essential failing would still remain. The less industrialized nations are treated as backward, and are assumed by all to be climbing towards the heights of technological, consumer society. This view of progress is fundamentally flawed, with the wrong means being used to achieve the wrong ends.

Like the spreading deserts, disappearing forests and rapidly rising pollution, the squalid conditions of the shanty-town dwellers and rural landless labourers are the inevitable by-product of industrialization. Quite clearly it is not a simple choice between people and the environment as is sometimes claimed. In fact, ironically, it is in the few remaining pockets of undeveloped natural environments that most inhabitants have food, clean water, stable social structures and a basic dignity that 'progress' elsewhere has invariably destroyed.

Even if the economic and technological development of Taiwan and South Korea could be duplicated elsewhere, the consequences would destroy the biosphere. If all countries were like the industrialized world, global output would have to be well over 100 times that of 1979. The degree of resource depletion, pollution and environmental degradation would be overwhelming.

The problem, however, is not just environmental. Economic transformation has also created so much social dislocation that it has often produced a cultural backlash. The extremism of the Ayatollahs in Iran is very much the result of the industrialization pursued by the Shah's regime.

The Nigerian writer Jimoh Omo-Fadaka sums up the essential flaw in the conventional model of development: 'The main reason why one can predict that industrialization will not solve the problems of the Third World is that it has not even solved those of the rich countries, even though it occurred there under the best possible conditions.' The only hope for the world's poor is to change direction. Gandhi, for example, recognized the need to build upon the traditional skills and wisdom of village communities.

Today in the Third World people are fighting back to save both their livelihoods and their environments: pressure groups include Malaysia's Consumer Association of Penang, Sri Lanka's Sarvodaya movement, Kenya's Green Belt campaign, and India's Chipko movement. The Third World has great traditions on which to rebuild itself. From Javanese multi-storied gardens to the 'food forests' of the Chagga on Mount Kilimanjaro, there are examples of efficient and productive farming. Many architectural critics have praised the qualities of vernacular architecture in many parts of the Third World. Furthermore, contrary to popular belief, many traditional societies successfully controlled their population size until outside interference disrupted their customs and culture. Once the pressure of exploitation is lifted, the countries of the Third World will be able to find their own solutions to their problems.

REAL AID TO THE POOR

The Third World matters to rich countries in many ways. Poverty is driving its victims to destroy their environments in the battle for survival; the consequent disruption of the planet's ecological stability could be disastrous. Inequality is increasing tensions and the danger of more wars which, in turn, could trigger superpower conflict. The indebtedness of many poor countries is threatening world financial stability. We all need Third World products. Such reasons appeal to basic self-interest. Yet many of the world's poor are powerless to threaten anyone — we should help reduce their suffering simply because it is the right thing to do.

At best, most political parties promise to increase aid (their record inspires little confidence) and to reduce the burden of debt on the poorest countries. This is in fact already happening as a face-saving operation disguised as generosity, since the debtor countries would otherwise default. As we have seen, as a response it is quite inadequate.

The Green approach goes to the root of the problem. It suggests an immediate ban on any involvement, financial or otherwise, in large dams, cattle ranching and similar projects in the Third World. At the same time, the big banks would be brought under control, as otherwise their power to create money and lend it to Third World countries would perpetuate financial chaos. A Green government would also withdraw from international institutions, including various agencies of the United

Nations, since their main role is to propagate the technology and culture of industrialism around the world.

In the short term, resources, especially those now spent on weaponry, should be made available to finance emergency measures like the universal provision of a clean water supply. As far as possible, funds should be channelled through relief agencies working with local organizations dedicated to the improvement of basic facilities in villages and urban slum areas. Beyond that, any assistance to Third World governments should be conditional on population control policies and on the protection of local natural environments and tribal peoples.

This might be seen as interference in the sovereignty of these nations. However, all aid is a form of intervention. It can never be neutral, and these requirements are essential for global well-being, something which overrides national self-interest. Obviously, without a halt to population growth, all other measures are put in jeopardy. Within the developed world, Green economic policies such as the turnover tax (penalizing companies of excessive size) offer a way to break up the corporate empires at the centre of so much exploitation in the Third World.

Past loans, from governments and financial institutions, should be used to protect tropical forests, mangrove swamps and other wildlife habitats in the Third World. Debts should be written off in return for the conservation of these regions, as well as the ecological rehabilitation of devastated areas. The justice of this scheme is that it is in the interests of rich and poor countries alike (as well as myriad other species). It is vital that these arrangements are carefully planned to avoid the mistakes typified by the Korup National Park in West Africa. Its creation not only displaced local tribal people but left the forest outside its boundaries unprotected.

In the long run, decisive change depends on rich countries relying more on their own resources and lowering their levels of population and consumption. This would allow Third World countries to retain more of their resources and to use them to satisfy their own needs. It would also facilitate social reform by undermining the economic base of many of the Third World's oppressive ruling élites. Special care would have to be taken so that the countries dependent on the export of one kind of commodity could make the transition without short-term damage to their economic well-being. Once done, however, there is every chance of lifting the scourge of global poverty.

20.
AT THE
CROSSROADS

Humanity has reached a point in its history which is as significant as the dawn of agriculture or the industrial revolution. We cannot go on as before: society and environment alike are beginning to break down. Greens are, however, not the only group to be proposing a way out of this crisis.

Inside various intellectual 'think tanks' or the co-ordinating forums of such élites as the Trilateral Commission, another vision of the future is emerging — superindustrialism. It is, essentially, an attempt to maintain 'business as usual' by means of the latest technologies and by the super-efficient management of people and physical resources. It pins its hopes on science and technology, and in particular on nuclear fusion, artificial intelligence, genetic engineering and, in the longer term, space colonization.

Writers such as Jeremy Rifkin have shown that technologies such as genetic engineering cannot evade the basic biophysical laws of nature. Their very efficiency is purchased at the expense of greater socio-ecological disorder in the world at large. The greatest danger from the superindustrialist vision is not any particular hazard, great though each individually may be. It is that we humans will reduce ourselves — and other species — to little more than mechanical cogs in a technological and social structure far beyond our comprehension and control.

ANYTHING GOES?

Superindustrialism may well find its ideological underpinnings in one of the more interesting theories from contemporary science, the Gaia hypothesis developed by James Lovelock and his associates. This bears a superficial resemblance to the age-old notion of an Earth Mother, and is concerned with the planet's ecological processes.

However, it also provides a legitimate excuse to seek, in the words of Teilhard de Chardin, 'to seize the tiller of creation'. An increasing number of writers and thinkers describe themselves as 'legitimate children of Gaia' to justify manipulation of the environment as well as of our own genetic make-up.

These intellectual trends are paralleled by social developments which journalist Tom Wolfe once summed up in the phrase the 'Me Decade'. This is characterized by introspection and self-absorption. Some writers take such narcissism to the extreme of denying that individuals should ever deserve shame or reproach (how would this be viewed by the victims of the Holocaust?). What is celebrated as an inner voyage of discovery might also be the voice of despair and surrender in the face of the triad of technology, business and government. More and more people seem to be turning their backs on the problems of society and environment, preferring the solitary contemplation of their own minds and bodies to the exclusion of all other concerns — which is exactly the kind of citizenry that superindustrialism will require.

A DANGEROUS FUTURE

The Green vision and that of superindustrialism are clearly incompatible, and the choice between them will be the real issue facing society — not the political divisions of Left and Right.

Superindustrialism is a far cry from any genuine struggle to build a free society in control of its institutions and its technologies, based, in Aldo Leopold's words, on 'a land ethic which changes the role of *Homo sapiens* from conqueror of the landcommunity to plain member and citizen of it'. Instead these selfstyled 'futurists' dream up seductive images of life in orbiting space cities. The reality of superindustrialism, be it under capitalism or communism, is likely to be rather different — more like Aldous Huxley's dreadful vision of totally manipulated human units, passively carrying out their predestined roles.

Huxley also had another vision, of a human-scale society in harmony with both itself and the rest of nature. This is the essence of the Green alternative.

THE ECOLOGICAL ALTERNATIVE

A Green programme is the only sensible way out of our current dilemmas, and there are no insurmountable technical obstacles to the construction of what we have called the ecosociety. Many of the technologies it would employ are proven, while the institutions needed for a 'steady-state' economy are in essence perfectly feasible. With the right political preparation, it would not be hard to gain public support for the measures entailed, since a Green reconstruction of society would offer the majority of people the opportunity for much more meaning and fulfilment in their lives.

The challenge, of course, is not to try to turn the clock back to some idealized state of bliss. Rather it is to find our own ways of achieving a new reconciliation between people and planet, taking advantage of all relevant developments in contemporary culture, science and technology. Yet in one sense it will of necessity involve a return to nature. A Green society would base itself upon the features found in undisturbed ecosystems — diversity, a multiplicity of niches, efficient energy use, the recycling of materials — to produce a resilient and satisfying new civilization.

DELAYING TACTICS

A favourite device for avoiding change is to call for more research. As Nobel prizewinner George Wald observes, 'if our world is coming to an end, set up a well-funded Project Apocalypse ... We are told that "all the facts are not yet in". How inane! All the facts are never in ... We already know enough to begin to cope with all the major problems that are now threatening human life and much of the rest of life on Earth. Our crisis is not a crisis of information; it is a crisis of decision, of policy.' Dr Wald's call was made some years ago, yet we are now even further from facing the real challenge of the future.

EMPTY EXPLANATIONS

The lack of action is often blamed on the media. Left-wing people accuse the media of being right-wing, while right-wing people make exactly the opposite accusation. In fact the mass media reflect public consciousness as much as they shape it.

Television might well sedate its viewers into passivity, and set the framework and agenda through which debate takes place, yet neither it nor the press fires magic bullets to brainwash viewers and readers.

There have been some excellent programmes on television about many of the issues covered in this book — with little apparent lasting effect. Yet many valuable developments such as the 'wholefood diet' revolution, the peace movement, women's liberation, the new pride of minority groups, either came before media interest or took place in the face of media ridicule and hostility. We cannot simply blame the media for the hostility of large sections of the public to radical ideas — Green or otherwise.

ARE PEOPLE BEING MISLED?

Some feel there is popular support for root and branch change, but that this is being betrayed by 'traitor' leaders. Politics are reduced to an exposure of misdeeds, supposedly in order to open the eyes of the masses. This tactic is perhaps most common on the radical Left, and credits political leaders with far more influence than they actually possess. It also diminishes the capacity of ordinary people to make up their own minds.

Some anarchists paint glowing pictures of the struggles of 'the people' against those who would stifle their aspirations. For them, progressive change will come about spontaneously. But that is not happening. It is no more useful to pretend that the majority of people are yearning for the promised land than it is to view them as victims of bad leadership. Greens start by acknowledging that in general people are of their own volition thinking and doing things that run counter to the values we support.

MAKING DO

Change is threatening, and it often seems much easier to hope that the business of living can continue as usual. It is also less effort to leave responsibility to others, rather than exercise it for ourselves. The reality — actual or promised — of material goods, technological devices and institutional services has given rise to a popular belief that we can go on making adjustments for ever, rather than radically changing our ways.

We can also deny the need for change by lowering our expectations, instead of recognizing how far standards have fallen. People find comfort in the sighting of a returned species of fish in a river, ignoring the fact that our rivers are in general unfit to drink or bathe in, and the reasons why that is so.

Our apparent adaptation to the industrial growth society can easily be confused with long-term stability. Professor René Dubos has observed: 'Millions upon millions of human beings who have developed in the urban and industrial environment are no longer aware of the stench of automobile exhausts or of the ugliness generated by the urban sprawl ... Life in the technologized environment seems to prove that man can become adapted to starless skies, treeless avenues, shapeless buildings, tasteless bread, joyless celebrations, spiritless pleasures — to a life without reverence for the past, love for the present, or poetical anticipation of the future.'

Yet, though people might want to cling to what they know best, change — not necessarily beneficial change — is coming. Our increasingly synthetic and uniform social and physical environment makes it questionable, according to Professor Dubos, whether 'man can retain his physical and mental health if he loses contact with the natural forces that have shaped his biological and mental nature'. And this 'surrogate' world is, as already discussed, fast undermining the capacity of the environment to support it.

HOPE FOR THE FUTURE?

Our problems do not just happen. They are not acts of God before which we are helpless. We still have the capacity to heal the dangerous wounds in our relations with each other and with our environment.

The antagonisms within societies and between human society and the rest of nature go back much further than industrialism. It is, for example, a myth that environmental exploitation is merely the flip side of social oppression. Free and classless societies have perpetrated great environmental destruction. Many technologies have been developed to serve human needs, yet have caused more problems than they solved. It is only too easy to doubt the possibility of building a Green society.

Yet many small-scale tribal communities *have* lived in equilibrium with their surrounding environment and its non-human inhabitants. Many of them were (and, in a few remote places, still are) free from most of the social vices that afflict modern 'civilization'. Their existence — covering the bulk of our time on Earth — refutes pessimistic interpretations of human nature. Anthropologists such as Colin Turnbull have shown that humans have the potential for better ways of living.

At the same time, Greens must recognize the darker side of our history. Indeed, it is this reality that makes the adoption of smaller institutions and softer technologies so urgent. It is tempting to think that present structures are somehow immutable. Yet settled farming societies, let alone the mass urban and industrial ones of today, are relatively recent innovations. The 'oil age' will probably cover only a handful of generations. There is no reason to think that humans cannot and will not change their way of living once again.

THE DYNAMICS OF CHANGE

Change results from a combination of factors. The crucial moment is when the balance of forces tips in favour of a rising movement for social change, and against the resistance of vested interests entrenched in the old order. Many people have an enormous stake in keeping things as they are — not just businessmen and politicians, but often their 'loyal servants' among society's lower ranks. Many of these gain a sense of security from knowing their place, while others dream of making their own way up the social ladder.

The cohesion of ruling élites can prove decisive. The power of big business and government might seem an insurmountable obstacle. Yet there is a kind of social entropy by which even the most formidable power structures decline and degenerate. Such bastions of established order as the Roman Empire, the feudal aristocracy and the European monarchies waxed and waned.

There are many signs that today's establishment is on the wane. There are specific battles being waged — women's rights, peace and environmental issues, trade unions, ethnic minorities and civil liberties. But more potent still is that deepening sense of unease across all of society, even the privileged, about the basic assumptions underlying the direction we are taking. Our rulers often seem lost for answers, desperately invoking such ideals as a restoration of 'traditional values'.

The other essential ingredient for positive change is the participation of those with a vision of a better society. Some of the most dramatic developments to date started from the work and dedication of tiny and insignificant minorities. They often faced apathy and repression, yet great changes in society bear testimony to what can be achieved. The mass labour movements around the world today were started by small bodies of dedicated people. Similarly, many individuals and groups are already working for a Green society.

21.
FROM HERE TO THERE

The emergence of the Green movement is the most promising political development in recent years. It ranges from individual researchers, philosophers and writers to pressure groups and new political parties. It includes many people who in one way or another are taking the future into their own hands by changing the way they live. This diversity is important. If one avenue of change is blocked or proves fruitless, there always remains scope for progress on other fronts.

Differences of emphasis can nevertheless conceal differences over basic values and direction. Glossing over them can sow the seeds of subsequent discord. The destructive in-fighting that has sometimes characterized Die Grünen, the German Green Party, should be a warning. We must recognize genuine divergences, while retaining a willingness to work together towards common ends. In conclusion, this last chapter considers how individuals convinced of the need for a Green society might best devote their time and energy to achieving it.

NEW LIVES FOR OLD

Lifestyle change can be very valuable. Major developments such as female self-emancipation would not have taken place without sufficient individuals deciding not to live as before. Our economic system is not yet so monolithic that enlightened choices are impossible. In many areas of living it is possible to be socially and ecologically more responsible. Books such as Kit Pedler's *Quest for Gaia* or John Seymour and Herbert Girardet's *Blueprint for a Green Planet* offer many suggestions. Personal change in diet can lead to better health, less cost and more enjoyment. We can also force change — many firms have reacted quickly to threats of consumer boycotts.

It is important to avoid the charge of hypocrisy. Non-converts will not be persuaded by those who talk of change but do nothing to alter their own lives. Non-converts are even less likely to be won over if we cannot point to some evidence that there is a practical alternative. We must recognize that real change is not an event but a process. There will never be the Green equivalent of 1917 and the Bolshevik Revolution. Changed lifestyles matter now, not at some date in the future. If people won't change their behaviour, a Green government will be as effective as Prohibition was against alcohol.

On the other hand, changing the institutional framework around us will help to make personal change easier, more successful and more likely. Changing individuals and changing society are different sides of the same coin, and each reflects and encourages the other.

WORKING FROM WITHIN

Some argue we should 'change the system from inside'. Radicals taking up senior posts in institutions such as industrial enterprises and government bodies often claim they are swapping impotence for influence. While not disputing the sincerity of many such ambitions, we should not forget that groups like employers have long been drawing the teeth of effective trade unionists by the judicious use of promotion. Individuals adapt to new circumstances, and few are strong enough to retain their former convictions.

PUTTING ON THE PRESSURE

Many sympathizers with Green ideas recognize that organized collective effort is necessary. A majority probably prefer to avoid identification with any political party, concentrating on single issue campaigns. Every desirable change helps, and environmental, peace, minority rights and social welfare campaigners can claim many positive achievements.

Single-issue politics, however, disguises the comprehensive and systemic nature of our ills by concentrating upon a particular malfunction. By focusing on symptoms such as nuclear power, it can mask root causes such as our high-energy society. It tends to focus upon individual decisions, whereas what matters most is the total system of decision-making in society — who is taking what decisions, how and why?

Broader and longer-term goals are sometimes sacrificed for the sake of influencing what may be only the margins of policy. That influence may be bought at the price of pulling punches, or not naming names. When members of these groups are co-opted on to committees the illusion is heightened that something is being done, though nothing fundamental may have changed. Single-issue campaigns often face a diminishing rate of return — membership and public interest slip away the longer the specific campaign goes on. Unlike political parties, they cannot easily switch to more populist avenues.

Influence in the corridors of power can be won by expertise, charismatic leaders or a group's size. All three tend to produce organizational structures which may relegate the rank and file membership to the role of supporters. Some single-issue campaigning pursues unity through the lowest common denominator, to increase membership.

The fear of alienating potential supporters can lead to serious problems of policy and action. The demands made by these campaigns often pose more questions than they answer, playing down vital aspects of the issue. Anti-nuclear compaigns often support demands for more coal-burning in order to curry favour with the mining industry, while many world development groups evade the population issue.

DIRECT AND TO THE POINT

Many evils have been spotlighted by successful direct actions such as blockades and publicity stunts. Some issues, however, do not offer such a high profile and self-contained objective as a nuclear reprocessing plant or a whaling ship, and so do not lend themselves to direct action. The law-breaking that may result creates hostages to fortune. If one group claims a moral justification to act illegally, it would be inconsistent to deny it to others.

GREENING THE OPPOSITION PARTIES

What about the political approach? Politics is dominated by the traditional parties of Left, Right and Centre. Their size can mesmerize us into thinking that the most hopeful way forward lies in converting them to a greener hue. It is a well-trodden path that has taken many radicals into the ranks of the major parties.

Perhaps the most significant have been socialists joining the left-wing parties. Guilt about their social circumstances often makes middle-class Marxists join what is seen to be a proletarian organization, and sentiments about the class struggle often seem to be strongest among those furthest removed from the factory floor.

Sometimes organized groups as well as individuals enter the larger parties. This can provide some salutary lessons. The Byzantine world of secret cabals often becomes an end in itself. Plotting to get through some resolution at the next local party meeting serves as a political playground for those weary of the all-too-real difficulties of achieving actual change.

Greens become familiar with the siren song sung by mainstream politics. It goes something like this: 'Yes, you people do have a point. But we've been in existence for decades, evolving all the time. We can take your ideas on board if you'd only join us and help change our party. You're wasting your time otherwise.' When radicals join an existing party, what tends to happen is that the party surreptitiously 'enters' them, slowly but surely changing how they think and act until there is little left of their original motivation. These 'entrists' soon end up as prisoners of the very machine they hoped to influence.

There are many reasons why socialist parties do not change, including their historical perspective, their base in the old industrial heartlands and their dependence on the trade union bureaucracy. They are political dinosaurs dragged down by the weight of their own structures, and self-perpetuation rather than the changing of society has become their chief reason for continued existence.

ECOSOCIALISM — A CONTRADICTION IN TERMS

Mainstream opposition to the *status quo* has mostly come from the socialist tradition. There is growing support for the idea of ecosocialism, a fusing of the Red and the Green, either inside or outside existing parties. Any such marriage is, however, likely to end in a quick divorce. Socialism is blinkered by its theory and practice from seeing the full scale of humanity's predicaments and how they may be resolved. It is not so much the failed track record of these parties once in office; writers such as Rudolph Bahro and André Gorz have shown the flaws in some of the basic assumptions underlying socialism's many faces.

Socialists have traditionally regarded capitalism as the root of all evil. Greens agree with much of what they say about capitalist economics, yet many sources of our ills either predate or have no necessary connection with capitalism. Left-wing ideology has not disputed the size and ingredients of the economic cake, arguing merely over how it should be sliced up. It shows no signs of recognizing that our problems start with the quantity and quality of the productive forces themselves. Indeed, to meet all the socialist promises would require even greater destructive demands on our resources. Fair shares in extinction might be equitable, but as a political statement of faith, it is not the Green way.

THE MIDDLE WAY?

Claiming to offer an alternative to socialism are the parties of the so-called centre of politics. Do they provide a more promising vehicle? While they claim the middle ground between Left and Right, they occupy the same part of the political spectrum as socialists and conservatives on the key issues of population control, 'steady-state' economics, a rejection of 'hard' technologies, and a reconciliation with the rest of nature. For many of them the 1950s represent their ideal — the very period when, as prescient individuals such as William Vogt, Fairfield Osborn and Samuel Ordway warned, society was quickening its pace down the wrong path. There is, however, a tradition of decentralist thinking among some of these parties which does offer a point of contact with the Green approach.

LESSER EVILS?

Many view the centre and left-wing parties as a lesser evil when compared with the unashamed politics of self-interest exhibited by right-wing politicians. Stopping right-wing governments from gaining office becomes the only priority at election times, and Greens have been accused of splitting the opposition vote. This leads to a call for tactical voting in favour of candidates best placed to beat those from the parties they dislike.

There have been occasions when such an effort could prove vital. Keeping out Hitler and the Nazis in the German elections of the early 1930s was one example. Yet what could be a useful tactic cannot be the basis for long-term strategy. The notion of a disciplined tactical vote depends upon large numbers voting in exactly the same 'correct' way — an unlikely occurrence.

Usually politics based on choosing the lesser of evils produces disappointment, and throws radical forces into disarray. In France, President Mitterand quickly dashed the hopes of those, including anti-nuclear campaigners, who argued that he would be an improvement on his more conservative rivals. The election in Britain of the Wilson/Callaghan government after that of Mr Heath produced few benefits, and in many ways prepared the way for Mrs Thatcher. Many current policies, from tied aid to secret rearmament programmes, were in fact pioneered by those who denounce them today.

The failures cannot be blamed on the personal deficiencies of opposition leaders once they get into power, but stem from the overall political framework. This leads to promises of thousands of new jobs when the real problem is to restructure the means by which people find a livelihood, or undertakings on environmental conservation while trying to promote more economic growth. Tactical voting and collaboration help to perpetuate the myths of conventional thinking. The real task is the opposite — to change the ways in which society thinks about, values and does things.

Recent history has shown that the successes achieved by 'purist' Green parties are in fact more likely to effect changes in mainstream parties than working from within them, or making compromises such as standing down at election time.

THE CASE FOR GREEN POLITICS

The political door to a better world can only be opened by changing the institutions that mould what individuals can and cannot do. If mainstream parties will not face that task, there is another option — the building of independent Green parties. This is happening in more and more countries.

Politics cannot be seen just in terms of marking a cross on a ballot paper every few years. Decisions to stand for election are only of tactical significance within a much broader approach. This seeks the agreement of like-minded people to work together for agreed goals based on a coherent set of principles. These are the essential foundations for a thorough diagnosis of society's problems and the formulation of an appropriate programme of institutional change.

Since the centres of power and influence are widespread, a party seriously interested in changing society needs to operate within as many fields as possible. Apart from elections to the various levels of government, the stronger the party becomes the more it will contest posts in trade unions, single-issue campaigns, professional bodies and community organizations — wherever Green policies might be pursued. It will put its views from whatever platforms are available, from local planning enquiries to the mass media, from street stalls to neighbourhood newsletters.

In the long run a successful Green party would have groups of members working to spread Green ideas and policies in all kinds of social, economic and cultural bodies, as well as 'purely political' ones. Successful ruling élites make no distinctions between the political and non-political, operating in pursuit of their common goals across many fronts.

PROSPECTS FOR SUCCESS

Green parties have recently been growing at an unprecedented rate, yet they remain tiny compared to the tasks they have set themselves. Large sections of the public have still not even heard of them. The situation is worse in countries such as Britain, where the 'first past the post' electoral system discriminates against new parties, with their support spread widely but thinly across the country.

Many otherwise sympathetic observers have concluded that the concept of Green politics is unrealistic. In periods of great change, however, 'realists' are often the furthest from what is the emerging reality. Examples abound in history of individuals and groups suddenly thrust out of what seemed the wilderness by the pace of events — Luther and Calvin during the Reformation, the radical parliamentarians during the reign of Charles I, the slavery abolitionists in the USA in the late 1850s and early '60s, the Bolsheviks in 1917, through to the radical right in the late 1970s.

Developments are currently at work which could transform the political landscape overnight. It might be a breakdown in the world financial system, or a catastrophic technological accident. It is impossible to predict such occurrences, yet we have seen there are many time-bombs ticking away beneath the industrial growth society. Though events may suddenly offer an opportunity for the Green parties, there is no guarantee that we will benefit from the changed circumstances. This will depend upon at least three key factors — clarity of vision, quality of organization, and deftness of strategy.

Greens have made considerable progress in the depth and breadth of their thought. There is now an impressive, fast expanding literature demonstrating a practical Green approach to problems in one field after another. Much work remains to be done regarding the finer points of detail and the mechanics of implementation; nevertheless, the rudiments of a working agenda for social and environmental regeneration are in place. The development of a broad programme is the next step, and we hope this book is a useful contribution towards that. Political activity otherwise becomes rudderless, trailing the fashions of the moment.

Fine ideas, however, have no future if confined to small circles of the converted. It takes organization and strategy to translate them into a potent force for winning over non-converts. This could prove the Achilles Heel of the Green parties. Perhaps as a reaction against the bureaucratic orthodoxies and even corruption of mainstream politics, Greens have so far proved incapable of forging organizations which would harness the skills and enthusiasms of their members, and make effective interventions in the real world outside the conference halls.

Greens are too often content to set up shop and wait for the customers to come in. As yet, there has been little organized campaigning, with specific policies aimed at specific audiences. Greens are not yet relating to the real hopes and fears of the people whose support could make a Green society something more than just talk.

ORGANIZE!

Greens will not make significant headway without efficient organization. Working in an organized way for democratically agreed targets increases the power of what individuals can achieve on their own. It also provides support and development, which individuals need to sustain and enrich their commitment. *Ad hoc* arrangements between committed and experienced individuals have a value. But they cannot substitute for the stable framework that good organization can provide, for disseminating knowledge, skills and experience to where they are needed.

Political commitment is about giving to others as well as taking from them. Greens need to overcome any reservations about the idea of leadership. Central co-ordination is necessary because of the unevenness of awareness, commitment and ability within any group. The dangers of undemocratic abuses are greatest in those bodies which lack proper structures to control the 'hand on the duplicator'. Principles such as accountability and recall can help to harmonize efficiency and democracy.

Green parties are not an embryo of future Green society but, rather, tools with which to intervene in the society of today. To be effective, the cut and thrust of rigorous internal debate is essential. Without it, wrong policies will never be put right, and members will not be properly briefed to argue their case in the face of hostile opponents from other parties.

145

Green parties cannot be safe havens providing a political retreat for those distressed by the bleak realities outside.

THE POLITICS OF THE FUTURE

The major parties usually have identifiable social constituencies from which they draw their support. Greens tap no particular vested interest, and potentially this is a great strength. Greens appeal to those aspects of human character which can be found within the majority of people. Often they are buried by force of circumstance. Even if dormant, however, they are still there. Most people want a better future for their children, free from the stains on our social and physical landscapes. Most people do not want the destruction we have catalogued in this book.

The task of Greens is to harness this revolutionary potential. To succeed, Greens need the energies and talents of sympathizers who now sit on the fence. It is not enough to wish the Greens well and then hold back from giving them the support that only active participation can provide.

People who are sympathetic to the ideas in this book must be prepared to help take the lead, to challenge the prevailing system and its grip on public values. In every forum, Greens need your support to contest and use positions of influence and authority in society. Change in individual lifestyles is an essential part of the process, but without control of the levers of power, it will be to no avail. None of us must turn away from this responsibility.

BIBLIOGRAPHY

A short book such as this is limited in what it can cover, and as a result many important issues have either been discussed only superficially or else left out altogether. This detailed bibliography should help to make amends and fill some of the gaps, while also providing supporting evidence for the views we have put forward. At the same time, and most importantly, it enables us to acknowledge our debt to the writers who have gone before us and on whose work we have widely drawn.

(Please note that the magazine articles recommended may be obtained through the inter-library loan system.)

THE ROAD TO RUIN

The dangers inherent in the present direction of society can be explored in:

Ehrlich, Paul and Anne. *Earth* (Thames Methuen, 1987). A brilliant portrayal of the depth and breadth of humanity's predicament.

Trainer, F.E. *Abandon Affluence* (Zed, 1985). Factual review of how society is hitting one barrier after another.

Seymour, John, and Girardet, Herbert. *Far From Paradise* (BBC, 1986). A wide-ranging, historical review of the maldevelopment of human society.

Miles, Ian, and Irvine, John, eds. *The Poverty of Progress* (Pergamon, 1982). A detailed look beneath the veneer of some of the world's richest countries.

Bunyard, Peter, and Morgan-Grenville, Fern. *The Green Alternative* (Methuen, 1987). In a question/answer format, a whole range of arguments are put forward to show why society must change its ways.

Miller, G. Tyler. *Living in the Enviroment* (Wadsworth, 1982). This provides a very accessible explanation of crucial sciences such as ecology and thermodynamics as well as a first-class discussion of many environmental and social issues.

Several writers issued early warnings of what was happening just after the Second World War. They are not only of historical interest but also demonstrate the flaws of other political traditions, whose framework of thinking blinded them to the dangers which they still play down or ignore. Look out for: Osborn, Fairfield. *Our Plundered*

Planet (Little Brown, 1948); Vogt, William. *The Road to Survival* (Sloane, 1948); Ordway, Samuel. *Resources and the American Dream* (Ronald Press, 1953).

Ehrlich, P., and Holdren, J., eds. *The Cassandra Conference: Resources and the Human Predicament* (Texas A&M Univ. Press, 1987). An anthology by people who, unfortunately, are entitled to say 'we told you so'.

See also:

Ehrlich, Paul, and Harriman, Richard. *How to be a Survivor* (Pan, 1971); Goldsmith, Edward, et al. *Blueprint for Survival* (Penguin, 1972); Meadows, D. et al. *The Limits to Growth* (Earth Island, 1972).

Some of the root causes of these predicaments are discussed in:

Goldsmith, Edward. 'Deindustrializing society', an article reprinted in a stimulating collection by the publisher of the leading independent Green magazine *The Ecologist*, entitled *The Great U-Turn* (Green Books, 1988).

Ehrlich, Paul, and Holdren, John. 'One-Dimensional Ecology' in *The Ecologist*, 1972, vol. 2, no. 2, p. 11-21. Perhaps the best demonstration of why it is wrong to blame our problems on any single factor or to play down the role of population growth and lifestyle choices.

Odum, Williams. 'Environmental Degradation and the Tyranny of Small Decisions', in *Bioscience*, Oct. 1972, vol. 32, no. 9, p. 728-729. A brief explanation of the way in which decisions made by individuals in their own immediate interest produce collectively disastrous results.

David Ehrenfeld, *The Arrogance of Humanism* (Oxford, 1981). A brilliant analysis of the costs of worshipping human reason, science and technological control.

Livingston, John, A. *One Cosmic Instant: Man's Fleeting Supremacy* (Houghton Mifflin, 1973). A study of human arrogance and its consequence for all species.

Berry, Wendell. *The Unsettling of America* (Sierra, 1977). Land abuse as an expression of a defective culture.

Capra, Fritjof. *The Turning Point* (Flamingo, 1983). A popular explanation of the harm caused by the mechanistic and supposedly 'value-free' ways of thinking that have dominated both the physical and social sciences.

Maxwell, Nicholas. 'Science, Reason, Knowledge and Wisdom: A Critique of Specialism', in *Inquiry*, 1980 23, p. 19-81. The dangers of hoping to find answers by simply accumulating more and more bits of knowledge.

Vickers, Geoffrey. 'The Weakness of Western Culture' in *Futures*, Dec. 1977, p. 457-473; and Jones, Thomas. 'Today's Obsolescent Aspirations' in *World Future Society Bulletin*, Nov.-Dec. 1979, p. 19-26: two overviews of the dangerous values underlying the industrial growth society.

BIBLIOGRAPHY

LIVING WITHIN LIMITS

On the ideology of 'progress':

Lyons, Dan. 'Are Luddites Confused?' in *Inquiry*, 1979, 22, p. 381-403. Why more know-how does not mean a better society.

Gomer, Robert. 'The Tyranny of Progress' in *Changing Perspectives on Man*, ed. B. Rothblatt (Univ. Chicago Press, 1968).

Hardin, Garrett. 'Ecology and the Death of Providence' in *Zygon*, 1980, 15, p. 57-6.

Orr, David. 'Modernization and the Ecological Perspective' in *The Global Predicament*, ed. Orr & Soroos (Univ. North Carolina Press, 1979).

Skolimowski, Henryk. 'The Myth of Progress' in *The Ecologist*, 1974, vol. 4, no. 7, p. 248-258.

Stent, Gunther. *The Paradoxes of Progress* (Freeman, 1978). A collection of articles on the theme of the self-limiting nature of 'progress', including intellectual advance.

Dubos, René. *The Dreams of Reason* (Columbia Univ. Press, 1961).

On the concept of limits to growth:

Ophuls, William. *Ecology and the Politics of Scarcity* (Freeman, 1977). The best single presentation of the limits to growth combined with an equally good explanation of the 'tragedy of the commons' (the cumulative consequences of individual decisions), though note the political reservations outlined in the Orr and Soroos volume (see above).

Miles, Rufus. *Awakening From the American Dream: The Social and Political Limits to Growth* (Marion Boyars, 1977). Explains the limits of managing increasingly complicated technologies and institutions. Particularly good on energy and food supply.

Davis, W. Jackson. *The Seventh Year: Industrial Society in Transition* (Norton, 1979). Why industrial civilization must decline.

Lovins, A.B. 'Long-Term Constraints on Human Activity' in *Environmental Conservation*, 1976, vol. 3, no. 1, p. 3-14.

Woodwell, G.M. 'Success, Succession, and Adam Smith' in *Bioscience*, Feb. 1974, p. 81-87. The failure of conventional economists and technologists to face ecological reality.

Hall, C.A.S. 'The Biosphere, the Industriosphere, and their Interactions' in *Bulletin of Atomic Scientists*, 1975, 31, p. 11-21.

Sears, P.B. 'The Inexorable Problem of Space' in *Science*, 1958, 127, p. 9-16.

Mathews, W.G. (ed.). *Outer Limits and Human Needs* (Dag Hammarskjold Foundation, 1976).

Watt, K.E.F. et al. *The Unsteady State: Environmental Problems, Growth and Culture* (Univ. Press of Hawaii, 1977). A critique of 'growthmania'.

Mishan, E.J. *Technology and Growth: The Price we Pay* (Praeger, 1970).

Pirages, Dennis, ed. *The Sustainable Society* (Praeger, 1977). A collection of articles exploring the limits to growth and their implications for society.

Burch, W.R., and Bormann. *Beyond Growth* (Yale, 1975). Another excellent collection on why we need a 'steady-state' society.

Rifkin, Jeremy. *Entropy* (Bantam, 1981). An easily digested explanation of this crucial concept and how policies that ignore it inevitably backfire.

Sale, Kirkpatrick. *Human Scale* (Secker & Warburg, 1980). The ills caused by the sheer size of our social and economic institutions are documented in compelling detail.

Elgin, D.S., and Bushnell, R.A. 'The Limits to Complexity' in *The Futurist*, Dec. 1977, p. 337-349. On the unmanageability of growing bureaucracies.

(Books and articles specifically on economic growth policies and the false assumptions of mainstream economic theory are listed later under 'Eco-nomics' while those on the social dissatisfactions and disruption caused by an expansionist system are listed under 'Consumerism'.)

Finally, on 'Limits', it is worth noting some excellent critiques of books epitomizing the faith that human society can continue its present course: Daly, Herman. 'Review of "Resourceful Earth"' (Simon, J., & Kahn, H., eds.) in *Bulletin of Atomic Scientists*, Jan. 1982, p. 39-42; Daly, Herman. 'The Ultimate Confusion' in *Futures*, October 1985, p. 446-450; Ehrlich, Paul. 'An Economist in Wonderland' in *Social Science Quarterly*, March 1981, vol. 62, no. 1, p. 44-49; Hardin, Garrett. 'The Born-Again Optimist' reprinted in a collection of articles by Hardin, *Naked Emperors* (Kaufmann, 1982); Bunyard, Peter. 'Global 2000 — Revisited' in *The Ecologist*, 1983, vol. 13, no. 4, p. 110-113.

SOME BASIC PRINCIPLES

Devall, Bill, and Sessions, George. *Deep Ecology: Living as if Nature Mattered* (Gibbs M. Smith/Peregrine Books, 1985). State of the art presentation of Green philosophy.

Porritt, Jonathon. *Seeing Green* (Blackwell, 1984). Our book stands on the shoulders of this pioneering presentation of what the Green movement is all about.

Schultz, R., and Hughes, J. Donald, eds. *Ecological Consciousness* (Univ. Press of America, 1981); Finnin, W.M., and Smith, G.A., eds. *Morality and Scarcity* (Louisiana State Univ. Press, 1979); Shepard, Paul, and McKinley, Daniel, eds. *The Subversive Science: Essays Towards an Ecology of Man* (Houghton Mifflin, 1969): three excellent collections.

Leopold, Aldo. *A Sand County Almanac* (O.U.P., 1968), the classic statement of the 'Land Ethic', and Callicott, J. Baird. *Companion to a Sand County Almanac* (Univ. of Wisconsin Press, 1987).

See also:

Berman, Morris. *The Reenchantment of the World* (Cornell Univ. Press, 1981).

Roszak, Theodore. *Where the Wasteland Ends* (Doubleday, 1973).

Birch, Charles, and Cobb, J.B. *The Liberation of Life* (Cambridge Univ. Press, 1974).

Rothenberg, David. 'A Platform of Deep Ecology' in *The Environmentalist*, 1987, vol. 7, no. 3, p. 185-190.

Kvaloy, Sigmund, 'Ecophilosophy and Ecopolitics' in *North American Review*, Summer 1974, 260, p. 17-28.

Snyder, Gary. 'Wild, Sacred, Good Land' reprinted in *The Schumacher Lectures*, vol. 2 (Abacus, 1984).

Darling, Frank Fraser, and Dasmann, Raymond. 'The Ecosystem View of Human Society' in *Impact of Science on Society*, 1969, vol. XIX, 2, p. 109-121.

Naess, Arne. 'A Defence of the Deep Ecology Movement' in *Environmental Ethics*, Fall 1984, vol. 6, p. 265-270.

Routley, Richard and Val. 'Human Chauvinism and Environmental Ethics' in *Environmental Philosophy*, ed. D. Mannison et al. (Australian Nat. Univ. Press, 1980).

Callicott, J. Baird. 'The Metaphysical Implications of Ecology' in *Environmental Ethics*, Winter 1986, vol, 8, p. 301-316.

POPULATION TIME BOMB

McGraw, Eric. *Population Misconceptions* (Population Concern, 1984). A short pamphlet which demolishes many myths on the subject, many of which circulate in 'radical' world development groups.

Catton, W.R. *Overshoot: The Ecological Basis of Revolutionary Change* (Univ. of Illinois Press, 1980). A good overview of this fundamental problem.

Borgstrom, Georg. *Too Many* (Collier-Macmillan, 1967).

Specific arguments are taken up in:

Ehrlich, Paul, and Holdren, John. 'Population and Panaceas' in *Bioscience*, Dec. 1969, vol. 19, no. 12, p. 1065-1071.

Ehrlich, Paul. 'Human Population and Environmental Problems' in *Environmental Conservation*, Spring 1974, vol. 1, no. 1, p. 15-20.

Ehrlich, Paul, and Holdren, John. 'The Human Population and the Global Environment' in *American Scientist*, May-June 1974, vol. 62, p. 282-292.

Ehrlich, Paul and Anne. 'The Dangers of Uninformed Optimism' in *Environmental Conservation*, Autumn 1981, vol. 89, no. 3, p. 173-175.

Teitelbaum, M.S. 'The Relevance of Demographic Transition Theory for Developing Countries' in *Science*, 1975, vol. 188, p. 420-425.

Hardin, Garrett. 'Beyond 1976: Can Americans be Well Nourished in a Starving World?' in *Annals, New York Academy of Sciences*, 1977, vol. 300, p. 87-91.

Hardin, Garrett. 'Population Skeletons in the Environmental Closet' in his collection *Stalking the Wild Taboo* (Kaufmann, 1978).

Hardin, Garrett. 'Cash Crops and Redistribution' and 'Conservation's Secret Question' both in *Naked Emperors*, op cit.

Eckholm, Eric. *Losing Ground: Environmental Stresses and World Food Prospects* (Norton, 1976)

Pimentel, David et al. 'Energy and Land Constraints in Food Protein Production in *Science*, 21 Nov. 1975, vol. 190, p. 754-760.

Pimentel, David, et al. 'Land Degradation: Effects on Food and Energy Resources' in *Science*, 8 Oct. 1976, vol. 194, p. 149-155.

Jensen, Neal. 'Limits to Growth in World Food Production' in *Science*, 28 July 1978, vol. 201, p. 317-320.

Odum, Eugene. 'Optimum Population and Environment' in *Current History*, June 1970, p. 355-359 and 365.

Wisnewski, R.L. 'Carrying Capacity: Understanding our Biological Limitations' in *Humboldt Jnl of Social Relations*, 1980, 7, 2, p. 55-70.

Day, Lincoln H. 'Concerning the Optimum Level of Population' in *Is There An Optimum Level of Population*, F. Singer, ed. (McGraw-Hill, 1971)

Tanton, John. 'International Migration as an Obstacle to Achieving World Stability' in *The Ecologist*, 1976, vol. 6, no. 6, p. 221-228.

Davis, Kingsley. 'Zero Population Growth: The Goal and the Means' in *Daedalus*, 1973, vol. 102, no. 2, p. 15-390.

The American Worldwatch Institute has published three excellent pamphlets on population policy: *Promoting Population Stabilization* (J. Jacobsen), *Women and Population Growth* (K. Newland) and *Men and Family Planning* (B. Stokes).

SUSTAINABLE SUPPLIES AND THE BIG CLEAN-UP

Murdoch, W.M. *Environment: Resources, Pollution and Society* (Snauer, 1975). An excellent general collection.

Brown, L.R. *The Twenty-Ninth Day* and *Building a Sustainable Society* (both Norton, 1978 and 1981 respectively); Eckholm, Eric. *Down to Earth: Environment and Human Needs* (Pluto, 1982): overviews of what is happening to the organic and mineral resources essential to human well-being.

Polesznski, Dag. 'Waste Production and Overdevelopment' in *Jnl of Peace Research*, 1977, vol. XIV, no. 4, p. 285-297. A study of the nature and extent of overconsumption.

Packard, Vance. *The Waste Makers* (Penguin, 1963). A classic study of 'planned obsolescence' and other wastage.

North, Richard. *The Real Cost* (Chatto & Windus, 1986). A detailed look at the resources used and pollution generated in the production, consumption and disposal of a whole range of goods, from tea to jeans.

Bookchin, Murray. *Our Synthetic Environment* (Harper and Row, 1974); Carson, Rachel. *Silent Spring* (Penguin, 1962); Commoner, Barry. *The Closing Circle* (Knopf, 1971): three classic studies of pollution.

Bent, Harry. 'Haste Makes Waste: Pollution and Entropy' in *Chemistry*, 1971, vol. 44, p. 6-15; Goldsmith, Edward. 'Can We Control Pollution?' reprinted in *The Great U-Turn* (op. cit.); two important reviews of the nature of pollution in industrial society.

Bryson, R.A., and Murray, T.J. *Climates of Hunger* (Univ. of Wisconsin, 1977). Though excessively focusing on one variable, this is an excellent portrayal of the dangers of human-caused climatic change and what must be done to minimize them.

Goldsmith, Edward, and Hildyard, Nicholas. *Green Britain or Industrial Wasteland* (Polity Press, 1986). A comprehensive survey of environmental degradation and pollution in the UK, spotlighting the repeated failure and frequent complicity of government agencies and 'establishment' scientists.

Hildyard, Nicholas. *Cover-Up* (N.E.L., 1983). Well-documented exposure of official cover-ups, ranging from bland denials and suppression of evidence to criminal acts in assorted pollution scandals.

See also:

Hekstra, G.P. 'Impact of Global Pollutants on Climate and Ecosystems' in *Ecoscript* 29, 1985.

McCormick, John. *Acid Earth* (Earthscan, 1985).

Bunyard, Peter. 'The Death of the Trees' in *The Ecologist*, 1986, vol. 16, no. 1, p. 4-13.

Hildyard, Nicholas, and Epstein, Samuel. *The Toxic Timebomb* (O.U.P., 1987).

Brown, Michael. *Laying Waste: The Poisoning of America* (Pantheon, 1980).

Pickaver, A. *The Pollution of the North Sea* (Greenpeace, 1981).

Dudley, Nigel. *This Poisoned Earth: The Truth about Pesticides* (Piatkus, 1987).

Panati, C., and Hudson, D. *The Silent Intruder: Surviving the Radiation Age* (Pan, 1982).

General books on practical ways of saving resources and reducing environmental damage include:

Seymour, John, and Girardet, Herbert. *Blueprint for a Green Planet* (Dorling Kindersley, 1987)

Button, John. *Green Pages: A Directory of Natural Products, Services, Resources and Ideas* (Optima, 1988).

Pedlar, Kit. *The Quest for Gaia* (Granada, 1979).

Hayes, Denis. *Repairs, Reuse, Recycling* (Worldwatch Institute, 1978).

Thomas, Christine. *Material Gains* (Earth Resources Research, 1979).

Vogler, John. *Work from Waste* (Intermediate Technology, 1981).

Friends of the Earth Handbook, ed. J. Porritt (Optima, 1987).

Trainer, F.E. 'How Cheaply Can We Live?' in *Ekistics*, Jan./Feb. 1984, vol. 304, p. 61-65. A survey of how groups of Australians have deliberately adopted lifestyles at much lower levels of consumption than the national average.

(References to the institutional aspects of resource conservation and pollution control are listed under 'Eco-nomics'. See also Appropriate Technology under 'Power Points')

PROTECTING THE WEB OF LIFE

Ehrlich, Paul and Anne. *Extinction* (Gollanz, 1981). The best single survey of the causes and consequences of the disappearing diversity of plants and animals.

Durrell, Lee. *State of the Ark* (Bodley Head, 1986). Broad-ranging survey with many well illustrated case studies.

See also:

Dorst, Jean. *Before Nature Dies* (Houghton Mifflin, 1970).

BIBLIOGRAPHY

Harte, John, and Socolow, Robert. *Patient Earth* (H.R.W., 1971).
Myers, Norman. *The Sinking Ark* (Pergamon, 1979).
Ehrenfeld, David. *Biological Conservation* (H.R.W., 1970).
Lamb, Robert. *World Without Trees* (Wildwood, 1979).
Grainger, Alan. *Desertification* (Earthscan, 1983).
Whyte, W. *The Last Landscape* (Doubleday, 1968).

On the specific costs of the extension and intensification of food, fibre, and timber production:

Kiley-Worthington, M. 'Problems of Modern Agriculture' in *Food Policy*, Aug. 1980, p. 208-215.
Fox, Michael. *Agricide* (Schocken, 1987).
Pimentel, D., and Terzune, E. 'Energy and Food' in *Annual Review of Energy*, 1977, 2, p. 171-195.
Reichert, W. 'Agriculture's Diminishing Diversity' in *Environment*, 1982, 24: 9, p. 6-11 and 39-43.
Shoard, M. *The Theft of the Countryside* (Temple Smith, 1980).
Pye-Smith, Charlie, and Rose, Chris. *Crisis and Conservation* (Penguin, 1984).
Mansolt, Sicco. *The Common Agricultural Policy* (Soil Association, 1979).
Ferguson, N. and D. *Sacred Cows at the Public Trough* (Maverick, 1983).
Hekstra, G.P. 'The Green Revolution Confronted with the World Conservation Strategy' in *Ecoscript* 14, 1982.
Wood, Nancy. *Clearcut: The Deforestation of America* (Sierra, 1971).
Grove, R. *The Future for Forestry* (BANC, 1983).
Stewart, P.J. *Growing Against The Grain: UK Forestry Policy* (CPRE, 1987).

On water resources and related engineering projects:

Goldsmith, Edward, and Hildyard, Nicholas. *The Social and Environmental Effects of Large Dams* (Wadebridge Ecological Centre, 1984). A three-volume study of the disastrous impact of large-scale irrigation and hydroelectric schemes, with many case studies.
Chandler, W. *The Myth of the TVA* (Environmental Policy Institute). Study of the Thirties scheme often held up as a model for the future.
Pearce, Fred. *Watershed* (Junction, 1982). Critique of British water management industry.

The fundamental significance of this destruction for human society is spotlighted in:

Odum, Eugene and Howard. 'Natural Areas as Necessary Components of Man's Total Environment' in *Transactions of the North American Wildlife Conference*, 1972, p. 178-189.
Bormann, F.H. 'An Inseparable Linkage: Conservation of Natural Ecosystems and the Conservation of Fossil Energy' in *Bioscience*, Dec. 1976, vol. 26, no. 12, p. 754-760.
Ehrlich, Paul. 'Variety is the Key to Life' in *Technology Review*, March/April 1980, p. 59-68.

Pimentel, David, et al. 'Environmental Quality and Natural Biota' in *Bioscience*, Nov. 1980, vol. 30. no. 11, p. 750-755.

Ehrlich, Paul. 'Human Carrying Capacity, Extinctions and Nature Reserves' in *Bioscience*, May, 1982, vol. 32, no. 5, p. 331-333.

Ehrlich, Paul, and Mooney, H.A. 'Extinction, Substitution and Ecosystem Services' in *Bioscience*, April 1983, vol. 33, no. 4, p. 248-254.

Iltis, H.H., et al. 'Criteria for an Optimum Human Environment' in *Bulletin of the Atomic Scientists*, 1970, 26:1, p. 2-6.

Martin, Vance, ed. *Wilderness* (Findhorn Press, 1982).

On the limitations to and contradictions of official environmental protection and, more generally, of 'resourcism', the utilitarian approach to the land and other species, see:

Livingston, John. *The Fallacy of Wildlife Conservation* (McClelland & Stewart, 1981).

Evernden, Neil. *The Natural Alien* (Univ. of Toronto Press, 1986).

Ehrenfeld, David. 'The Conservation of Non-Resources' in *American Scientist*, Nov.-Dec. 1976, p. 648-656.

Devall, Bill, and Sessions, George. 'The Development of Natural Resources and the Conservation of Nature' in *Environmental Ethics*, Winter 1984, vol. 6, p. 293-322.

Hays, Samuel. *Conservation and the Gospel of Efficiency* (Harvard, 1959).

On more specific failures of mainstream environmental management:

Macinko, George. 'Saturation: A Problem Avoided in Planning Land Use' in *Science*, 30 July, 1965, vol. 149, p. 516-521.

Weijden, W.J., et al. 'Nature Conservation and Agricultural Policy in the Netherlands' in *Ecologist Quarterly*, Winter 1978, p. 317-335.

Dustin, Daniel, and McAvoy, Leo. 'Hardening the National Parks' in *Environmental Ethics*, Spring 1980, vol. 2, p. 39-44.

MacEwen, Ann and Malcolm. 'Nature and Landscape: Why the Great Divide?' in *Ecos*, 1981, 2(2), p. 24-29.

MacEwan, Ann and Malcolm. *National Parks: Conservation or Cosmetics?* (Allen & Unwin, 1982).

Selman, Paul. 'Environmental Conservation or Countryside Cosmetics?' in *The Ecologist*, 1976, vol. 6, no. 9, p. 333-335.

Adams, W.R. *Nature's Place, Conservation Sites and Countryside Change* (Allen & Unwin, 1986).

Kreith, F. 'Lack of Impact' (The American National Environmental Policy Act) in *Environment*, Jan/Feb. 1973, vol. 15, no. 1, p. 26-33.

Shrader-Frechette, K.S. 'Environmental Impact Assessment and the Fallacy of Unfinished Business' in *Environmental Ethics*, Spring 1982, vol. 4, p. 37-47.

Lang, Reg. 'Environmental Impact Assessment' in *Ecology Versus Politics*, ed. W. Leiss (Univ. of Toronto, 1979).

Pearce, D. 'The Limits of Cost-Benefit Analysis as a Guide to Environmental Policy' in *Kyklos*, 1976, vol. 29, no. 1, p. 97-112.

Animal rights: The prime requirement of non-human species is somewhere to flourish, and habitat destruction therefore poses the gravest threat. However, human abuse of other creatures is nothing if not varied, ranging from the abattoir to the vivisection lab. and zoos. Here we list some of the many books now calling for an end to such practices:

Singer, Peter, ed. *In Defence of Animals* (Blackwell, 1985).

However, making other species 'honorary humans' has its contradictions and a greener approach to the issue is to be found in:
Callicott, J.Baird. 'Animal Liberation: A Triangular Affair' in *Environmental Ethics*, Winter 1980, vol. 2, p. 311-338.
Rodman, John. 'The Liberation of Nature?' in *Inquiry*, 1977, 20, p. 83-131.

On more appropriate forms of land use, see:

Jackson, W. et al. *Meeting the Expectations of the Land* (N. Point Press, 1984).
Coates, G., ed. *Resettling America* (Brick House, 1981).
Jackson, Wes. *New Roots for Agriculture* (Univ. of Nebraska Press, 1985).
Conviser, Richard. 'Towards Agricultures of Context' in *Environmental Ethics*, 1984, 6, p. 71-85.
Altieri, Miguel. *Agroecology* (Westview, 1986).
Lockeretz, W., ed. *Environmentally Sound Agriculture* (Praeger, 1983).
Stonehouse, B., ed. *Biological Husbandry* (Butterworth, 1981).
Kiley-Worthington. 'Ecological Agriculture: What it is and how it Works' in *Agriculture and Environment*, 1981, 6, p. 349-381.
Mollison, Bill. *Permaculture One* and *Two* (I. T. C. I, 1981, and Tagari, 1979).
Hodges, R.D. 'The Case for Biological Agriculture' in *Ecologist Quarterly*, Summer 1978, p. 122-143.
Boeringa. R., ed. *Alternative Methods of Agriculture* (Elsevier, 1980).
Berry, Wendell. *The Gift of Good Land* (North Point Press, 1981).
Merrill, Richard, ed. *Radical Agriculture* (New York Univ. Press, 1976).
Pye-Smith, Charlie, and North, Richard. *Working the Land* (Temple Smith, 1984).
Pye-Smith, C., and Hall, C. *The Countryside We Want* (Green Books, 1987).
Raphael, Ray. *Tree Talk: People and Politics of Timber* (Island, 1981). Includes critique of the lumber industry as well as descriptions of 'holistic forestry'.
Douglas, J.S., and Hart, R. *Forest Farming* (Intermediate Technology, 1985).
Hart, R. *The Forest Garden* (Institute for Social Inventions, 1987). One man's achievement.
Grainger, Alan. 'Reafforesting Britain' in *The Ecologist*, 1981, vol. 11, no. 2, p. 54-81. General plan for restoration of what has long been destroyed.
Coleman, A. 'Place of Forestry in a Viable Land Use Strategy' in *Quarterly Jnl of Forestry*, 1980, vol. 84, no. 1, p. 20-29.

BIBLIOGRAPHY

Mutch, W.E.S. 'Combined Land Use at Fassfern' in *International Tree Crops Jnl*, 1980, 1, p. 49-60. Case study from the Scottish Highlands.

Smyser, Carol et al. *Nature's Design: A Practical Guide to Natural Landscaping* (Rodale, 1982).

Riley, P.J., and Warren, D.S. 'Money Down the Drain: A Rational Approach to Sewage' in *The Ecologist*, Dec. 1980, vol. 10, no. 10, p. 342-345.

On greening the city:

Corbett, Michael. *A Better Place to Live: New Designs for Tomorrow's Communities* (Rodale, 1982).

Ryn, S van der, and Calthorpe, P. *Sustainable Communities* (Sierra).

Morris, David. *Self-Reliant Cities* (Sierra, 1982).

Britz, R., et al. *The Edible City Resource Manual* (Kaufmann, 1981).

On land ownership, taxation, and planning, see:

Shoard, Marion. *This Land is our Land* (Paladin, 1987).

Girardet, Herbert, ed., *Land for the People* (Crescent Books, 1976).

Harrison, F. *Land Tenure* (Paper to The Other Economic Summit, London, 1984).

Green Party Economics Group. *Community Ground Rent Brief* (1987).

McHarg, Ian. *Design with Nature* (Doubleday, 1969).

McHarg, Ian. 'Human Ecological Planning' in *Landscape Planning*, 1981, 8:2, p. 109-120.

Johnson, A.H. et al. 'A Case Study in Ecological Planning' in *Agronomy Jnl*, 1979, 21, p. 935-955.

Five examples of 'transitional' measures for an industrialized country like Britain are offered in: *Proposals for a Natural Heritage Bill* (Friends of the Earth, 1983); Potter, Clive. *Investing in Rural Harmony* (World Wildlife Fund/UK, 1983); Sinclair, G. *How to Help Farmers and Keep England Beautiful* (C.P.R.E. and Council For National Parks, 1985); MacEwan, Malcolm, and Sinclair, G. *New Life for the Hills* (C.N.P., 1983); *Hill Farming and Birds: A Survival Plan* (R.S.P.B., 1984).

POWER POINTS

On the limits to technology:

Schwartz, Eugene. *Overskill* (Ballantine, 1971). A classic study of why technological answers are part of the problem.

Rifkin, J. *Declarations of a Heretic* (RKP, 1985). Assault on technocratic thinking, including a lucid explanation of why new superstar technologies such as genetic engineering do not overcome the ecological and entropic limits to growth.

Mumford, L. *The Myth of the Machine* (Harcourt, 1970).

Ferkiss, V. *Technological Man.* (Braziller, 1969).

Watt, K.E.F. *The Titanic Effect* (Sinauer, 1974).

McDermott, J. 'Technology: The Opiate of the Intellectuals' in *New York Review of Books*, 31 July 1969.

Waters, W.B. 'Landing a Man Downtown' in *Bulletin of Atomic Scientists*, 1973, 29(9), 34-35, How problems down on Earth differ from those tackled by the space programme.

Holdren, John. 'Technology, Environment and Well-Being' in *Growth in America*, ed. C. Cooper (Westview, 1976). Explodes major technocratic fantasies.

Giarini, O., and Louberge, H. *The Diminishing Returns to Technology* (Pergamon, 1979).

Lowrance, W. *Of Acceptable Risk* (Kaufmann, 1976). Problems of determining safety.

On appropriate technology and design:

Drengson, A.R. 'Toward a Philosophy of Appropriate Technology' in *Humboldt Jnl of Social Relations*, 1982, vol. 9, no. 2, p. 161-176.

Winner, Langdon 'The Political Philosophy of Alternative Technology' in *Technology in Society*, 1979, vol. 1, p. 75-86.

Todd, J. and N. *Tomorrow is our Permanent Address* (Harper & Row, 1980).

Todd, J. and N. *Bioshelters, Ocean Arks, City Farming: Ecology as the Basis of Design* (Sierra, 1984).

Dorf, R.C., and Hunter, Y.L., eds. *Appropriate Visions* (Boyd & Fraeser, 1978).

Illich, Ivan. *Tools for Conviviality* (Calder & Boyars, 1973).

McRobie, George. *Small is Possible* (Abacus, 1982).

Alexander, C., et al. *A Pattern Language* (O.U.P., 1977).

Papanek, Victor. *Design for the Real World* (Granada, 1974). How to design things to save resources and serve people.

On the energy problem:

Budnitz, R. and Holdren, J. 'Social and Environmental Costs of Energy Systems' in *Annual Review of Energy*, 1976, 1, p. 553-580.

Daly, H. 'On Thinking About Energy' in *Natural Resources Forum*, 1978, 3, p. 19-26.

Woodwell, G.M. 'Short-circuiting the Cheap Power Fantasy' in *Natural History Magazine*, Oct. 1974.

Lovins, A.B. *World Energy Strategies* (Ballinger, 1975).

Lovins, A.B. 'Re-examining the Nature of the EEC Energy Problem' in *Energy Policy*, Sept. 1979, p. 178-198.

Lovins, A.B. 'Limits to Energy Conversion' in *Alternatives to Growth 1*, ed. D. Meadows (Ballinger, 1977).

Holdren, J., et al. 'Energy: Calculating the Risks' in *Science*, 1979, May 11, no. 204, p. 564-68.

Lovins, A. 'Cost-Risk-Benefit Assessments in Energy Policy' in *George Washington Law Review*, Aug. 1977, vol. 45, no. 5, p. 911-943.

On fossil fuels, see above and also:

Taylor, Vince. 'The End of The Oil Age' in *The Ecologist*, Oct/Nov. 1980, vol. 10, no. 8/9, p. 303-311.

Wales Ecology Party. *Coal and Economic Growth* (1984).

Dials, G., and Moore, E. 'The Cost of Coal' in *Environment*, 1974, 16: 7, p. 30-37.

BIBLIOGRAPHY

Brown, W. 'The Rape of Black Mesa' and Davis, W. 'The Stripmining of America', both in *Voices for the Earth*, A. Gilliam, ed. (Sierra, 1981).

McCaull, J. 'Wringing out the West' in *Environment*, 1974, 16: 7, p. 10-17. Reveals the foolishness of thinking that there are vast reserves of coal simply waiting to be tapped.

On nuclear energy:

Valentine, J. *Atomic Crossroads* (Merlin, 1985).

Jeffery, J. 'The Unique Dangers of Nuclear Power' in *The Ecologist*, 1986, vol. 16, no. 4/5, p. 147-163.

Bertell, Rosalie. *No Immediate Danger* (Women's Press, 1985).

Gofman, J. *Radiation and Health* (Sierra, 1981).

Tolstoy, Ivan. 'High Level Waste: No Technical Solution' in *The Ecologist*, 1986, vol. 16, no. 4/5, p. 205-209.

Bartlett, D., and Steele, J. *Forevermore: Nuclear Waste in America* (Norton, 1985).

Bunyard, P. 'Nuclear Power — The Grand Illusion' in *The Ecologist*, 1980, vol. 10, no. 4, p. 116-130.

Sweet, C. *The Price of Nuclear Power* (Heinemann, 1983).

Bunyard, P. 'The Myth of France's Cheap Nuclear Electricity' and Jeffery, J.W. 'The Collapse of Nuclear Economies', both in *The Ecologist*, 1988, vol. 18, no. 1, p. 4-13.

Pringle, P., and Spigelman, J. *The Nuclear Barons* (Sphere, 1983).

Patterson, W. *The Fissile Society* (Earth Resources Research, 1977).

Durie, S., and Edwards, R. *Fuelling the Nuclear Arms Race* (Pluto, 1982).

Appropriate energy:

Trainer, F.E. 'Limitations of Alternative Energy Sources' in *Conservation and Recycling*, 1984, 7: 1, p. 27-42.

Holdren, J. et al. 'Environmental Aspects of Renewable Energy Sources' in *Annual Review of Energy*, 1980, vol. 5, p. 241-291.

Mackillop, A., and Bunyard, P. 'The Wrong Alternatives' in *The New Ecologist*, Mar./Apr. 1978, no. 2, p. 42-46.

Pimental, D., et al. 'The Environmental and Social Costs of Biomass Energy' in *Bioscience*, Feb. 1984, vol. 34., no. 2, p. 89-94.

Taylor, G. Rattray. 'Tidal Barrages: Boon or Blight?' in *The Ecologist*, 1980, vol. 10, no. 5, p. 167-169.

Lovins, A. and L.H. *Brittle Power* (Brick House, 1982) and *Energy Unbound* (Sierra, 1986). The first book demonstrates how, because of their intrinsic resilience, alternative sources of energy offer greater security than large centralized schemes. The second takes the form of a novel, sorting out appropriate and inappropriate alternative sources of energy. Like many of their books, these two suffer from a naive faith in unfettered market forces.

Socolow, R. 'The Coming Age of Conservation' in *Annual Review of Energy*, 1977, 2, p. 239-289.

McDaniel, B. 'Economic and Social Foundations of Solar Energy' in *Environmental Ethics*, Summer 1983, p. 155-168.

Clark, W. 'Renewable Energy Sources and a Conservation Economy' in *The Ecologist*, 1977, vol. 7, no. 7, p. 283-296.

Lovins, A.B. *Soft Energy Paths* (Harper & Row, 1979).

Nash, H. *Soft Path Questions and Answers* (Brick House, 1979).

Lovins, A. and L.H. *Least-Cost Energy: Solving the Carbon Dioxide Problem* (Brick House, 1982).

Steinhart, J., et al. *Pathway to Energy Sufficiency* (F.O.E./America, 1979).

Leach, G. et al. *A Low Energy Strategy for the UK* (I.I.E.D., 1979).

Sorenson, B. Energy and Resources, in *Science*, 25 July 1975, vol. 189, p. 255-260. Case study of how Denmark could meet its needs from solar sources.

Flavin, C. *Electricity from Sunlight* (Worldwatch Institute, 1982).

Flavin, C. *Energy and Architecture* (Worldwatch Institute, 1980).

Jenkins, N. 'Combined Heat and Power' in *The Ecologist*, 1986, vol. 16, no. 4/5, p. 213-216.

Hannon, B. 'Energy Conservation and the Consumer' in *Science*, 1975, vol. 189, p. 95-102.

Daneker, G. *Energy, Jobs and Economy* (Alyson, 1979).

Ridgeway, J. *Energy-Efficient Community Planning* (J.G. Press, 1980).

Okagaki, A., and Benson, J. *The County Energy Plan Guidebook* (Institute Ecologica, 1979).

On other technological issues:

COMPUTER TECHNOLOGY

Roszak, Theodore. *The Cult of Information: The Folklore of Computing and the True Art of Thinking* (Paladin, 1988).

Weizenbaum, J. *Computer Power and Human Reason: From Judgement to Calculation* (Penguin, 1984).

Dreyfus, Herbert. *What Computers Can't Do* (Harper & Row, 1972).

Shallice, Michael. *The Silicon Idol* (O.U.P., 1984).

Skolimowski, H. 'Information — Yes, but where has all our wisdom gone?' in *The Ecologist*, 1984, vol. 14, no. 506, p. 232-234.

TELEVISION

Large, Martin. *Who's Bringing them up?* (TV Action Group, 1980).

Winn, M. *The Plug-in Drug* (Bantam, 1978).

Emery, F. and M. *A Choice of Futures to Enlighten or to Inform* (Australian National Univ., 1975).

Mander, Jerry. *Four Arguments for the Elimination of Television* (Morrow Quill, 1977).

TRANSPORTATION

Rivers, Patrick. *The Restless Generation* (Davis-Poynter, 1972). What we sacrifice on the altar of the god of mobility.

Mumford, Lewis. *The Highway and the City* (H, B & W, 1963).

Hamer, M. *Wheels Within Wheels: a Study of the Road Lobby* (RKP, 1987). Spotlight on the web of vested interests that's getting us nowhere fast.

Plowden, Stephen, *Taming Traffic* (Andre Deutsch, 1980).

BIBLIOGRAPHY

SPACE PROGRAMME

Aldridge, A., and Skolimowski, H. 'Pie in the Sky: Do We Really Want Colonies in Space?' in *The Ecologist*, 1977, vol. 7, no. 10, p. 390-394.

Salmon, J.D. 'Resupplying Spaceship Earth: Prospects for Space Industrialization' (in Orr and Soroos, op. cit.).

Mumford, Lewis and Wald, George. 'Letters on Space Colonies' in *Co-Evolution Quarterly*, Spring 1976, p. 6, and 16-17 respectively.

ECO-NOMICS

On economic theory in general:

Georgescu-Roegen, N. *The Entropy Law of the Economic Process* (Harvard, 1971); Georgescu-Roegen, N. *Energy and Economic Myths* (Pergamon, 1977): two classic studies of the flawed assumptions beneath mainstream economic theorizing, from Marxism to monetarism. They shed light on a great many issues, not least the fact that 'sustainable growth' is a contradiction in terms.

See also:

Georgescu-Roegen, N. 'Methods in Economic Science' in *Jnl of Economic Issues*, June 1979, Vol. XIII, no. 2, p. 317-328.

Georgescu-Roegen, N. 'Mechanistic Dogma and Economics' in *Methodology and Science*, 1974, vol. 7, p. 174-184.

Daly, H. 'Steady-State Economics versus Growthmania: a critique of the orthodox conceptions of growth, wants, scarcity and efficiency' in *Policy Sciences*, 1974, 5, p. 149-167.

Daly, H. 'Thermodynamic and Economic Concepts' in *Land Economics*, 1986, vol. 62, no. 3, p. 319-322.

Daly, H. 'The Circular Flow of Exchange Value and the Linear Throughput of Matter-Energy' in *Review of Social Economy*, 1985, vol. 43, no. 3, p. 279-297.

Mishan, E.J. *Economic Myths and the Mythology of Economics* (Wheatsheaf, 1986).

Singh, Narindar. *Economics and the Crisis of Ecology* (O.U.P., 1978).

Hueting, R. *The New Scarcity and Economic Growth* (North-Holland, 1980).

Weisskopf, W.A. *Alienation and Economics* (Dutton, 1971).

Dieren, W. van, and Hummelinck, M.G. *Nature's Price: the Economics of Mother Earth* (Marion Boyars, 1979). Popular presentation of the dependence of any economic system upon ecological well-being, though flawed by an attempt to put cash prices upon the priceless.

Wilden, A. 'Ecosystems and Economic Systems' in *Cultures of the Future*, ed. M. Maruyama and A. Harkin (Moulton, 1978).

More specifically on economic growth policies:

Johnson, W.E., and Hardesty, J., eds. *Economic Growth and the Environment* (Wadsworth, 1971)

Daly, H. 'Growth Economics and the Fallacy of Misplaced Concreteness' in *American Behavioural Scientist*, 1980, vol. 24, no. 1, p. 79-105.

Mishan, E.J. *The Costs of Economic Growth* (Penguin, 1969).

Mishan, E.J. *The Economic Growth Debate* (Allen & Unwin, 1977).

Mishan, E.J. 'Whatever Happened to Progress?' in *Jnl of Economic Issues*, 1978, XII:2, p. 405-425.

Zolotas, X. *Economic Growth and Declining Social Welfare* (World Bank, 1981).

Parsons, Jack. *The Economic Transition* (Conservation Trust, 1975).

Hodson, H.V. *The Diseconomies of Growth* (Earth Island, 1977).

Leipart, C. *Economic Growth and its Social Costs* (Paper to The Other Economic Summit, London, 1985).

Boulding, Kenneth. 'Fun and Games with the Gross National Product' in *Environment and Society*, ed. D. Roelefs et al. (Prentice Hall, 1974).

Doeleman, J.A. 'On the Social Rate of Discount' in *Environmental Ethics*, Spring 1980, vol. 2, p. 45-48; Price, C. 'To the Future: With Indifference or Concern?' in *Jnl of Agricultural Economics*, 1973, 24, p. 393-397: two studies of the failure of present economic mechanisms to take account of the needs of posterity.

Daly, H. *Steady-State Economics* (Freeman, 1977). The best statement of why and how to build a steady-state economy.

Daly, H, ed. *Economics, Ecology, Ethics* (Freeman, 1980). The best collection of articles on the same theme.

Daly, H. 'Toward a New Economic Model' in *Bulletin of Atomic Scientists*, 1986, vol. 42, no. 4, p. 42-44.

Ayres, R.U. *Resources, Environment and Economics: Applications of the materials/energy-balance principle* (Krieger).

Galtung, J. *Towards a New Economics: on the theory and practice of self-reliance* (Conference paper, The Other Economic Summit, 1985).

Potma, T. *Consumers, Workers and Industry are Better off with an Environmentally Oriented Economy* (Paper to second Congress of European Greens, Dover, 1985).

Backstrand, Goran and Ingelstam. 'Should we put Limits on Consumption?' in *The Futurist*, June 1977, XI, p. 157-162.

Westman, W.E., and Gifford, R.M. 'Environmental Impact: controlling the overall level' in *Science*, 31 Aug. 73, vol. 181, 819-825.

Green Party Economics Working Group briefs on 'Taxation' and 'Money and Debt' (1987).

Weston, D. *Green Economics — The Community Use of Currency* (Paper to The Other Economic Summit, London, 1985).

Collard, D. *Altruism and Economy: a study in non-selfish economics* (O.U.P., 1978).

CONSUMERISM

On the assumptions underlying the faith in market forces and the willingness to pay as the basis of decision-making:

Sagoff, Mark. 'Do We Need a Land Use Ethic?' in *Environmental Ethics*, Winter 1981, vol. 3, p. 293-308.

Polyanyi, Karl. 'Our Obsolete Marker Mentality' in *The Ecologist*, 1974, vol. 4, no. 6, p. 213-220.

Meadows, Donella. 'Equity, the Free Market, and the Sustainable State' in *Alternatives to Growth*, 1, ed. D. Meadows, op. cit.
Sagoff, M. 'At the Shrine of Our Lady Fatima, or why political questions are not all economic' reprinted in *Earthbound*, ed. T. Regan (Temple Univ. Press, 1984).
Hines, L.G. *The Myth of Idle Resources* (Transaction of 18th North American Wildlife Conference, 1953, p. 28-35).
Kahn, A.E. 'Tyranny of Small Decisions' in *Kyklos*, 1968, no. 1, p. 23-47.
Schelling, T.C. 'On the Ecology of Micromotives' in *The Public Interest*, 1971, no. 25, p. 59-98.

On the dissatisfactions and self-cancelling effects of consumerism:

Various. 'Consumer Power' in *New Internationalist*, May 1985, p. 7-28.
Ewens, S. and E. *Channels of Desire* (McGraw Hill, 1982).
Leiss, William. *The Limits to Satisfaction* (Marion Boyars, 1978).
Hirsch, Fred. *The Social Limits to Growth* (RKP, 1978).
Scitovsky, Tibor. *The Joyless Economy* (O.U.P., 1976).
Linder, Steffan. *The Harried Leisure Class* (Columbia Univ. Press, 1970).

MAKING A LIVING

Braverman, H. *Labour and Monopoly Capital* (Monthly Review Press, 1974). What happens when human labour is treated as a mere commodity.
Handy, C. *The Future of Work* (Blackwell, 1985).
Osmond, J. *Work in the Future: Alternatives to Unemployment* (Thorsons, 1986).
Schumacher, F. *Good Work* (Abacus, 1979).
Gorz, A. *Paths to Paradise: On the Liberation from Work* (Pluto, 1985). Explorations by an independent French Marxist.
Miller, A. *The Economic Implications of Basic Income Schemes* (Paper to The Other Economic Summit, London, 1984).
Sparrow, P. *Unemployment and Unvalued Work: True Costs and Benefits* (Paper to The Other Economic Summit, London, 1985).
Barbier, E. *Earthworks: Environmental Approaches to Employment Creation* (F.O.E./UK, 1981).

REGIONAL DECLINE

Morris, D., and Hess, K. *Neighbourhood Power: the new localism* (Beacon, 1975).
Ross, D., and Usher, P. *From the Roots Up: economic development as if community mattered* (I.T.G., 1985).
Robertson, J. *The Economics of Local Recovery* (Paper to The Other Economic Summit, London, 1986).
Penney, K. *Aspects of Local Economic Self-Sufficiency* (Paper to The Other Economic Summit, London, 1984).
Various. 'Local Economic Regeneration and Co-Operation' in *The Living Economy*, ed. P. Ekins (RKP, 1986).

SHARING AND CARING

Davis, J., and Mauch, S. 'Strategies for Societal Development', Allen, R. 'Towards a Primary Life-Style' and Goldsmith, E. 'Settlements and Social Stability', all in *Alternatives to Growth* 1, ed. D. Meadows (op.cit.).

Drengson, A. 'Toward a Philosophy of Community' in *Philosophy Forum*, 1979, vol. 16, p. 101-125.

Brownell, Baker. *The Human Community* (Harper & Row, 1950).

Colwell, T.B. 'The Ecological Basis of Human Community' in *Educational Theory*, 1971, 21:4, p. 418-433.

For details of oppression and exploitation round the world:

Humana, Charles. *The Human Rights Guide* (Pan, 1987).

On the 'imperialism' of certain professional groups and bureaucracies within society:

Illich, Ivan et al. *Disabling Professions* (Marion Boyars, 1977).

Goodman, McKnight, John et al. 'Big Brother in a Box' in *The New Ecologist*, Sept./Oct. 1978, no. 5, p. 158-160.

Johns, Ruth. *Life Goes On* (Unknown Publisher — sic — 1982). More specific and practical study on the relationship between social problems, self-help projects and the official services based on the work of the Nottingham Family First Trust.

On the issue of the rights of ownership:

Stillman, P.G. 'Property Rights, Ecological Limits and the Steady-State' in *The Sustainable Society*, ed. D. Pirages, op.cit.

Two discussions of the frequently used argument that Green values are opposed to the interests of the less well-to-do:

Pope, Carl. 'Growth and the Poor' in *Sierra Club Bulletin*, 1975, 3, p. 7-11, 30-31. Evidence from America that more roads and more suburban sprawl increase social inequality.

Love, Sam. 'Ecology and Social Justice: is there a conflict?' in *Environment Action*, 1972, Aug. 5, p. 3-6. How the poor bear the worst burden of pollution.

On the individualistic culture of industrialism:

Lasch, C. 'Consumption, Narcissism and Mass Culture' in *The Minimal Self*, ed. C. Lasch (Picador, 1984).

Slater, P. *Earthwalk* (Doubleday, 1984).

Slater, P. *The Pursuit of Loneliness* (Beacon, 1970).

Merchant, Carolyn. 'Earthcare' in *Environment*, June 1981, vol. 23, no. 5, p. 6-40. Feminism has made a crucial contribution to the building of right relationships both within society and between society and the rest of nature. Patriarchical thinking and social structures are some of the oldest roots of our problems, something missed by those who exclusively blame them on this or that economic system. Merchant's article is a very good overview of these perspectives and contains numerous suggestions for follow-up reading.

On young people in our society:

Packard, V. *Our Endangered Children* (Little, Brown, 1983).

On arts, recreation and leisure:

Abbs, P. *The Black Rainbow: essays on the present breakdown of culture* (Heinemann, 1974).
Lane, J. *Death and Resurrection of the Arts* (Green Alliance, 1982)
Carlson, A. 'Nature and Positive Aesthetics' in *Environmental Ethics*, 1984, 6, p. 5-34.
Krippendorf, J. *The Holiday Makers: understanding the impact of leisure and travel* (Heinemann, 1987).
Simons, P. 'Apres Ski le Deluge' in *New Scientist*, 14, Jan. 1988, p. 49-52. Case study of the impact of a growing leisure pursuit.
Gardner, J., and Marsh, J. 'Recreation in Consumer and Conserver Societies' in *Alternatives*, 1978, 7, p. 25-29.

A ROOF OVER OUR HEADS

On general urban redevelopment and modern housing schemes:

Goodman, Robert. *After the Planners* (Penguin, 1972).
Ravetz, Alison. *Remaking Cities* (Croom Helm, 1980).
Davies, J.G. *The Evangelical Bureaucrat* (Tavistock, 1972).
Coleman, A. *Utopia on Trial* (Shipman, 1985).
Hildyard, N. 'Building for Collapse' in *The Ecologist*, 1977, vol. 7, no. 2, p.46-54.

On more community-centred programmes:
Turner, J. *Housing by People* (Marion Boyars, 1976).
Cassidy, R. *Livable Cities* (HRW, 1980).
Wates, N., and Knevitt, C. *Community Architecture* (Penguin, 1987).
Talbot, M. *Reviving Buildings and Communities* (David & Charles, 1986).

More specifically on individual buildings:

Ward, C. *When We Build Again* (Pluto).
Eccli, Eugene. *Low-Cost, Energy-Efficient Shelters* (Rodale, 1976).
Clarke, R. *Building for Self-Sufficiency* (Universe, 1977).

SCHOOL'S OUT?

North, Richard. *Schools of Tomorrow* (Green Books, 1987).
Grieg, S., et al. *Earthrights: Education as if the Planet Really Mattered* (WWF/Kogan Page, 1987).
Colwell, T. 'Significance of Ecology for the Philosophy of Education' in *Proceedings in the Philosophy of Education*, 1982, vol. 38, p. 177-185.
Clegg, A. and Megson, B. *Children in Distress* (Penguin, 1968).
Clegg, A. *About our Schools* (Blackwell, 1980).

GOOD NEIGHBOURS

Schell, J. *The Fate of the Earth* (Knopf, 1982). The dangers from the nuclear arsenals.

Rogers, P., et al. *As Lambs to Slaughter* (Arrow/Ecoropa, 1981).

Prins, G., ed. *Defended to Death* (Penguin, 1983).

White, A. *The Terror of Balance* (Menard Press, 1983).

Caldicott, H. *Missile Envy, the Arms Race and Nuclear War* (Bantam, 1985).

Garrison, J. *The Russian Threat* (Gateway, 1983). How we are kept in a state of deadly rivalry.

Barnett, A. *Iron Britannia* (Allison & Busby, 1982). The Falklands War put in the context of modern British society.

Dixon, N. *On the Psychology of Military Incompetence* (Futura, 1976); Regan, G. *Someone has Blundered* (Batsford): two studies that undermine any faith in the decision-making ability of the military-political establishment.

Boulding, Kenneth. 'Peace Against War' in *Human Ecology*, 1984, vol. 12, no. 2, p. 209-13.

Boulding, Kenneth. 'Perspectives on Violence' in *Zygon* Dec. 1983, vol. 18, no. 4, p. 425-437.

Ryle, M.H. *The Politics of Nuclear Disarmament* (Pluto, 1981).

Alternative Defence Commission. *Defence Without the Bomb* (Taylor & Francis, 1983).

Green CND. *Embrace the Earth: a Green View of Peace* (1983).

Barnet, R., and Muller, R. *Global Reach* (Simon & Schuster, 1974). The malign power of the transnational corporation.

Kohr, L. *The Breakdown of Nations* (RKP, 1957). Why and how states must be broken into smaller units.

Sale, K. *Dwellers in the Land: the bioregional vision* (Sierra, 1985). Ecodecentralism explained.

Goldsmith, E. 'Ethnocracy: the Lesson from Africa' in *The Ecologist*, 1980, vol. 10, no. 4, p. 134-140. The connection between conflict and boundaries that ignore ethnic and cultural realities.

Green Party. *Decentralization Brief* (1987).

Johnson, P. *Neutrality — a Policy for Britain* (Temple Smith, 1985).

GLOBAL POVERTY TRAP

Agarwal, Anil. *The State of the Environment and the Resulting State of 'The Last Person'* (World Wildlife Fund-UK, 1985). A powerful statement of how environmental destruction is at the expense of the world's poor, not for their wellbeing as claimed by those who want to industrialize the planet.

Hekstra, G.P. 'Development Policies Ignore Ecological Constraints' in *The Ecologist*, 1985, vol. 15, no. 5/6, p. 240-245. The impossibility of baking a 'bigger cake' as a solution for world poverty.

Farvar, M.T., and Milton, J.P., eds. *The Careless Technology: ecology and international development* (Natural History Press, 1972). A catalogue of misconceived projects.

Biswas, A.K., ed. *Climate and Development* (Tycooly, 1984). Some intrinsic climatic and ecological limits on the transfer of industrialized farming and Western-style development to tropical regions.

Hardin, Garrett. 'An Ecolate View of the Human Predicament' in *Alternatives*, 1981, vol. VII, 2, p. 242-262.

Hardin, Garrett. 'Limited World, Limited Rights' in *Society*, 1980, 17(4), p. 5-8. Necessary correctives to the excess rhetoric of 'One World', though Hardin's concept of 'Lifeboat Ethics' is based on bad history and false analogies.

Omo Fadaka, J. 'Industrialization and Poverty in the Third World' in *The Ecologist*, Feb. 1974, vol. 4, no. 2, 61-63.

Dumont, R. *Stranglehold on Africa* (Deutsch, 1983).

Goldsmith, E. 'Is Development the Solution or the Problem?' in *The Ecologist*, 1985, vol. 15, no. 5/5, p. 210-219.

Goldsmith, E. 'Dedeveloping the Third World' in *The Ecologist*, 1977, no. 7, p. 338-339.

Goldsmith, E. 'Open Letter to the President of the World Bank' in *The Ecologist*, 1985, vol. 15, no. 1/2, p. 4-8. Challenge to the thinking behind one of main agencies of global social and environmental destruction.

Burch, D. *Appropriate Technology for the Third World Development* (Griffin Univ. Press). Why technology transfer must be both culturally and environmentally appropriate.

Madeley, J. 'Does Economic Development Feed People?' in *The Ecologist*, 1985, vol. 15, no. 1/2, p. 36-41.

Dando, W. *The Geography of Famine* (Arnold, 1980). Roots of hunger in maldevelopment.

Jenkins, Robin. *The Road to Alto* (Pluto, 1979). The price of 'progress' for a traditional community in Portugal.

Esteva, Gustavo. 'Development Is Dangerous' in *Resurgence*, 1986, Jan./Feb., 114, p. 14-16.

Adams, P., and Solomon, L. *In the Name of Progress* (Energy Probe, 1985).

Bunyard, P. 'Can Self-sufficient Communities Survive the Onslaught of Development?' in *The Ecologist*, 1984, vol. 14, no. 1, p. 2-5.

Davis, S. *Victims of the Miracle* (C.U.P., 1977). The realities of Brazil's 'progress'.

Wehrheim, J. 'Paradise Lost' in *The Ecologist*, 1971, vol. 1, no. 10, p. 4-8. The impact of Americanization on Hawaii.

Various. 'Indonesia's Transmigration Programme' in *The Ecologist*, 1986, vol. 16, no. 2/3, p. 58-117.

Hayter, T. *The Creation of World Poverty* (Pluto, 1981). Spotlights the evasions and false assumptions behind the Brandt Report.

Marnham, P. *Fantastic Invasion* (Penguin, 1987); Rodney, W. *How Europe Underdeveloped Africa* (Bogle L'Ouverture, 1972): two studies of the maldevelopment of Africa before and after colonial independence.

On trade and aid:

Dumont, R., and Cohen, N. *The Growth of Hunger* (Marion Boyars, 1980).

Hensman, C.R. *Rich Against Poor* (Penguin, 1971).

Henderson, H. 'The Uneconomics of World Trade' in *Resurgence*, 1981, July/Aug., no. 87, p. 28-29.

Kent, G. 'Food Trade: the Poor Feed the Rich' in *The Ecologist*, 1985, vol. 15, no. 5/6, p. 232-239.

Curry-Lindahl, K. *Development Assistance with Responsibility* (Ecoscript 17, 1984).

Linear, M. *Zapping the Third World: The disaster of development aid* (Pluto, 1985).

Hayter, T., and Watson, C. *Aid: Rhetoric and Reality* (Pluto, 1981).

Eckholm, E. *The Dispossessed of the Earth: land reform and sustainable development* (Worldwatch, 1979).

Sachs, W. *Delinking from the World Market* (Paper to The Other Economic Summit, London, 1985).

Maathai, W. *The Kenyan Green Belt Movement* (Paper to The Other Economic Summit, London, 1985).

Kapur, J. 'India in the Year 2000 — A Vision' in *The Ecologist*, 1975, vol. 5, no. 8, p. 290-300.

Ariyaratne, A. 'No Poverty Society' in *Resurgence*, 1985, Jan./Feb., 108, p. 4-8.

Macy, J. *Dharma and Development* (Kumarian Press, 1983).

Bandyopadhyay, J., and Shiva, V. 'Chipko: Rekindling India's Forest Culture' in *The Ecologist*, 1987, vol. 17, no. 1, p. 26-34.

Various. 'Tropical Forests: Plan for Action' in *The Ecologist*, 1987, vol. 17, no. 4/5.

Fathy, H. *Architecture for the Poor* (Univ. of Chicago Press, 1973). Example of traditional skills within poor countries.

AT THE CROSSROADS

Dubos, Rene. *Man Adapting* (Yale, 1965). The dangers of our success in adapting to present lifestyles.

Goldsmith, Edward. 'High Technology Euphoria' (review of Peter Russell's *The Awakening Earth*) in *The Ecologist*, 1983, vol. 13, no. 5, p. 190-192.

Lasch, C. *The Culture of Narcissism* (Sphere, 1980).

Berman, Morris. 'The Cybernetic Dream of the 21st Century' in *Journal of Human Psychology*, 1986, 26:2, p. 24-51.

Rossman, Michael. *New Age Blues* (Heyday, 1984).

FROM HERE TO THERE

Hooker, C.A., and Hulst, R. van. 'Institutionalizing a High Quality Conserver Society' in *Alternatives*, Winter 1980, 9, p. 25-36. Why the central issue is political power and changing the institutional and technological framework of our lives.

Spretnak, C., and Capra, F. *Green Politics* (Paladin, 1985). A stimulating look at the problems to be overcome in building a Green political movement.

Dellinger, D. *More Power Than We Know* (Doubleday, 1975). Why radical minorities are often stronger than they think.

Sear, P. 'Utopia and the Living Landscape' in *Daedalus*, Spring 1965, vol. 94, no. 2. Eloquent statement of the relevance of utopian thinking.

Callenbach, Ernest. *Ecotopia Emerging* and *Ecotopia* (Bantam, 1977): two-part fictional visualization of the birth and functioning of a Green society.

Allsop, B. *Towards a Humane Architecture* (Frederick Muller, 1974).
Wells, M. *Gentle Architecture* (McGraw, 1982).

SAFE AND SOUND

Dossey, Larry. *Space, Time and Medicine* (Shambala, 1982).
Leshan, Lawrence. *Holistic Health* (Turnstone, 1984).
Illich, Ivan. *Limits to Medicine* (Penguin, 1977).
McKnight, J. *De-Medicalization and the Possibilities of Health* (Paper to The Other Economic Summit, London, 1985).
McKnight, J. 'The Politics of Medicine' in *New Ecologist*, July/Aug. 1978, no. 4, p. 112-114.
Armelagos, G., and Katz, P. 'Technology, Health and Disease in America' in *The Ecologist*, 1977, vol. 7, no. 7, p. 304-317.
Powles, J. 'The Medicine of Industrial Man' in *The Ecologist*, Oct. 1972, vol. 2, no. 10, p. 24-36.
Powles, J. 'Have Health Services Reduced Mortality?' in *The Ecologist*, 1977, vol. 7, no. 8, p. 303-310.
Boyden, S. 'Evolution and Health' in *The Ecologist*, 1973, vol. 3, no. 8, p. 304-309.
Kidel, M. 'The Challenge of Illness' in *Resurgence*, Jan/Feb. 1985, 108, p. 37-40.
Ehrenreich, B., and English, D. *For Her Own Good: 150 years of medical advice for women* (Pluto, 1979).
Epstein, S. *The Politics of Cancer* (Sierra, 1978).
Chowka, P.B. 'The Organized Drugging of America' in *The Ecologist*, Aug. 1979, vol. 9, no. 4/5, p. 155-160.
Inglis, Brian. *The Diseases of Civilization* (Hodder & Stoughton, 1981).
Melville, A., and Johnson, C. *Cured to Death* (Secker & Warburg, 1982).
Hall, Ross Hume *Food for Nought* (Doubleday, 1974).
Walker, Caroline, and Cannon, Geoffrey. *The Food Scandal* (Century, 1984).
Ehrlichman, James. *Gluttons for Punishment* (Penguin, 1986).
Wardle, Chris. *Changing Food Habits* (Earth Resources Research, 1977).
Millstone, Erik. *Food Additives* (Penguin, 1986).
Polunin, Miriam. *The Right Way to Eat* (Dent/Ecoropa, 1984).
Jones, A. 'Alternative Medicine — Alternative Society' in *The Ecologist*, 1984, vol. 14, no. 4, p. 156-160.
Mansfield, P. 'Doctors For the People' in *Resurgence*, Mar./Apr. 1985, 109,, p. 28-30.
Rosser, Jilly. 'Our Birthright' in *Resurgence*, Jan./Feb. 1984, p. 19-23).

INDEX